TH.

JANE AUSTEN

Selected from the Compilation of her
Great Nephew

EDWARD, LORD BRADBOURNE

By

SARAH CHAUNCEY WOOLSEY

First published in 1892

This edition published by Read Books Ltd.
Copyright © 2018 Read Books Ltd.
This book is copyright and may not be
reproduced or copied in any way without
the express permission of the publisher in writing

British Library Cataloguing-in-Publication Data
A catalogue record for this book is available
from the British Library

JANE AUSTEN

Jane Austen was an English novelist whose works of romantic fiction, set among the landed gentry, earned her a place as one of the most widely read writers in English literature. Her realism, biting irony and social commentary have gained her historical importance among the reading public, scholars and critics alike.

Austen was born on 16th December 1775, and lived her entire life as part of a close-knit family located on the lower fringes of the English landed gentry. Biographical information on Jane Austen is incredibly scarce however, as only some personal and family letters remain. She was educated primarily by her father and older brothers as well as through her own reading. Jane spent most of her early years being schooled at home, until leaving for boarding school at the age of ten, alongside her elder sister Cassandra. They left one year later though (1786) as the family could not afford to send both of their daughters to school. According to Park Honan, a biographer of Austen, life in the Austen home was lived in 'an open, amused, easy intellectual atmosphere' where the ideas of those with whom the Austens might disagree politically or socially were 'considered and discussed.' After returning from school in 1786, Austen 'never again lived anywhere beyond the bounds of her immediate family environment.'

Her artistic apprenticeship lasted from her teenage years into her thirties. As Austen grew into adulthood, she continued to live at her parents' home, carrying out those activities normal for women of her age and social standing: she practised the fortepiano, assisted her sister and mother with supervising servants, and attended female relatives during childbirth and older relatives on their deathbeds. During this period, she experimented with various literary forms, including the epistolary novel (a novel written as a series of documents) which she then abandoned, and wrote and extensively revised three major novels and began a fourth. *Lady Susan,* written between 1793 and 1795 was an experiment of this kind; taking the form of a series of letters, it is described as Austen's most ambitious and sophisticated early work. Austen biographer Claire Tomalin describes the heroine of the novella as a 'sexual predator who uses her intelligence and charm to manipulate, betray, and abuse her victims, whether lovers, friends or family.'

In 1800, George Austen (Jane's father), announced his decision to retire from his post in the ministry and move the family to Bath. Jane Austen was incredibly unsettled and unhappy in Bath, and sadly her father passed away during this period. This left the family in a precarious financial position and in 1805 Jane, her sisters and her mother lived in rented quarters. They moved to 'Chawton Cottage' in Hampshire in 1809. A gift from Austen's brother Edward, this cottage allowed the family a more settled life and in a quieter, more tranquil setting. Austen was thus able to concentrate on her writing. From 1811 until 1816, with the release of *Sense and Sensibility* (1811), *Pride and Prejudice* (1813), *Mansfield Park* (1814) and *Emma* (1815), she achieved success as a published writer.

Through her brother Henry, the publisher Thomas Egerton agreed to issue *Sense and Sensibility,* and the earnings from the novel provided Austen with some much needed financial and psychological independence. Egerton then published *Pride and Prejudice,* a revision of *First Impressions,* in January 1813. He advertised the book widely and it was an immediate success, garnering three favourable reviews and selling well. *Mansfield Park* followed, but was not popular, and the failure of this title offset most of the profits Austen earned on Emma. These were the last of Austen's novels to be published during her lifetime. She wrote two additional novels, *Northanger Abbey* and *Persuasion,* both published posthumously in 1818, and began a third, which was eventually titled *Sanditon,* but died before completing it.

Early in 1816, Jane Austen began to feel unwell. She ignored her illness at first and continued to work and to participate in the usual round of family activities. By the middle of that year, her decline was unmistakable to Austen and to her family, and Austen's physical condition began a long, slow deterioration, culminating in her death the following year. Some biographers assign her symptoms to Addison's disease, and others to Hodgkin's lymphoma or even bovine tuberculosis from drinking unpasteurised milk; she was weak and couldn't walk from stiff joints. Austen died in Winchester, whilst seeking medical treatment, on 18th July 1817, at the age of forty-one. She is buried in the north aisle of the nave of Winchester Cathedral.

Austen's works critique the novels of sensibility of the second half of the eighteenth century and are part of the transition to nineteenth century realism. Her plots, though fundamentally comic, highlight the dependence of women on marriage to secure social standing and economic security. Her works though usually popular, were first published anonymously and brought her little personal fame and only a few positive reviews during her lifetime. It was the publication in 1869 of her nephew's *A Memoir of Jane Austen* that introduced her to a wider public, and by the 1940s she had become widely accepted in academia as a great English writer. The second half of the twentieth century saw a proliferation of Austen scholarship and the emergence of a Janeite fan culture. Her novels are still well-read, studied and loved right up to the present day.

*From a Painting in the possession of the
Rev. Morland Rice, of Bramber.*

PREFACE

THE recent cult for Miss Austen, which has resulted in no less than ten new editions of her novels within a decade and three memoirs by different hands within as many years, have made the facts of her life familiar to most readers. It was a short life, and an uneventful one as viewed from the standpoint of our modern times, when steam and electricity have linked together the ends of the earth, and the very air seems teeming with news, agitations, discussions. We have barely time to recover our breath between post and post; and the morning paper with its statements of disaster and its hints of still greater evils to be, is scarcely out-lived, when, lo! in comes the evening issue, contradicting the news of the morning, to be sure, but full of omens and auguries of its own to strew our pillows with the seed of wakefulness.

To us, publications come hot and hot from the press. Telegraphic wires like the intricate and incalculable zigzags of the lightning ramify above our heads; and who can tell at what moment their[iv] darts may strike? In Miss Austen's day the tranquil, drowsy, decorous English day of a century since, all was different. News travelled then from hand to hand, carried in creaking post-wagons, or in cases of extreme urgency by men on horseback. When a gentleman journeying in his own "chaise" took three days in going from Exeter to London, a distance now covered in three hours of railroad, there was little chance of frequent surprises. Love, sorrow, and death were in the world then as now, and worked their will upon the sons of men; but people did not expect happenings every day or even every year. No doubt they lived the longer for this exemption from excitement, and kept their nerves in a state of wholesome repair; but it goes without saying that the events of which they knew so little did not stir them deeply.

Miss Austen's life coincided with two of the momentous epochs of history,—the American struggle for independence, and the French Revolution; but there is scarcely an allusion to either in her letters. She was interested in the fleet and its victories because two of her brothers were in the navy and had promotion and prize-money to look forward to. In this connection she mentions Trafalgar and the Egyptian expedition, and generously remarks that she would read Southey's "Life of Nelson" if there was anything in it about her brother Frank! She honors Sir John Moore by remarking after his death that his mother would perhaps have preferred to have him less distinguished and still alive; further than that, the making of the gooseberry jam and a good recipe for orange wine interests her more than all the marchings and countermarchings, the man[oe]uvres and diplomacies, going on the world over. In the midst of the universal vortex of fear and hope, triumph and defeat, while the fate of Britain and British liberty hung trembling in the balance, she sits writing her letters, trimming her caps, and discussing small beer with her sister in a lively and unruffled fashion wonderful to contemplate. "The society of rural England in those days," as Mr. Goldwin Smith happily puts it, "enjoyed a calm of its own in the midst of the European tempest like the windless centre of a circular storm."

The point of view of a woman with such an environment must naturally be circumscribed and narrow; and in this Miss Austen's charm consists. Seeing little, she painted what she saw with absolute fidelity and a dexterity and perfection unequalled. "On her was bestowed, though in a humble form, the gift which had been bestowed on Homer, Shakespeare, Cervantes, Scott, and a few others,—the gift of creative power." Endowed with the keenest and most delicate insight and a vivid sense of humor, she depicted with exactitude what she observed and what she understood, giving to each fact and emotion its precise shade and value. The things she did not see she did not attempt. Affectation was impossible to her,—most of all, affectation of knowledge or feeling not justly her own. "She held the mirror up to her time" with an exquisite sincerity and fidelity; and the closeness of her study brought her intimately near to those hidden springs which underlie all human nature. This is the reason why, for all their skimp skirts, leg-of-mutton sleeves, and bygone impossible bonnets, her characters do not seem to us old-fashioned. Minds and hearts are made pretty much after the same pattern from century to century; and given a modern dress and speech, Emma or Elizabeth or dear Anne Eliot could enter a drawing-room to-day, and excite no surprise except by so closely resembling the people whom they would find there.

"Miss Austen's novels are dateless things," Mr. Augustine Birrell tells us. "Nobody in his senses would speak of them as 'old novels.' 'John Inglesant' is an old novel, so is 'Ginx's Baby.' But Emma is quite new, and, like a wise woman, affords few clues to her age."

We allude with a special touch of affection to Anne Eliot. "Persuasion," which was written during the last two years of Miss Austen's life, when the refining touch of Eternity was already upon her, has always seemed to us the most perfect of her novels; and Anne, with her exquisite breeding and unselfish straightforwardness, just touched with the tender reserve of memory and regret, one of her best portraitures. But this is a matter of individual taste. Doubtless Elizabeth Bennet is "better fun" as the modern girl would say. Miss Austen herself preferred her. She had a droll and pretty way of talking about her characters which showed how real they were to her own mind, and made them equally real to other people. In 1813 she had the good luck to light upon a portrait of Jane Bennet at an exhibition.

"I was very well pleased (pray tell Fanny) with a small portrait of Mrs. Bingley, excessively like her. I went in hopes of seeing one of her sister, but there was no Mrs. Darcy. Perhaps I may find her in the great exhibition, which we shall go to if we have time. Mrs. Bingley's is exactly like herself,—size, shaped face, features and sweetness; there never was a greater likeness. She is dressed in a white gown, with green ornaments, which convinces me of what I had always supposed, that green was a favorite color with her. I dare say Mrs. D. will be in yellow."

And later:—

"We have been both to the exhibition and Sir J. Reynolds'; and I am disappointed, for there was nothing like Mrs. D. at either. I can only imagine that Mr. D. prizes any picture of her too much to like it should be exposed to the public eye. I can imagine he would have that sort of feeling,—that mixture of love, pride, and delicacy."

The letters included in this series comprise about three quarters of the collection in two volumes published in 1884 by her great-nephew Lord Brabourne. The lightness, almost friskiness, of their tone cannot fail to strike the reader. Modern letters written by women are filled more or less with hints and queries; questionings as to the why and the wherefore occur; allusions to the various "fads" of the day, literary or artistic,— Ibsen, Tolstoi, Browning, Esoteric Buddhism, Wagner's Music, the Mind Cure, Social Science, Causes and Reforms. But Cowper and Crabbe were the poetical sensations in Miss Austen's time, Scott and Byron its phenomenal novelties; it took months to get most books printed, and years to persuade anybody to read them. Furthermore the letters, in all probability, are carefully chosen to reveal only the more superficial side of their writer. There are wide gaps of omission, covering important events such as Mr. Austen's death, the long illness through which Jane nursed her brother Henry, and the anxieties and worries which his failure in business caused to the whole family. What is vouchsafed us is a glimpse of the girlish and untroubled moments of Miss Austen's life; and the glimpse is a sweet and friendly one. We are glad to have it, in spite of our suspicion that another and even more interesting part of her personality is withheld from us.

A good daughter, a delightful sister, the most perfect of aunts, what better record could there be of a single woman? Her literary work never stood in the way of her home duties, any more than her "quiet, limpid, unimpassioned style" stood between her thought and her readers.

Her fame may justly be said to be almost entirely posthumous. She was read and praised to a moderate degree during her lifetime, but all her novels together brought her no more than seven hundred pounds; and her reputation, as it were, was in its close-sheathed bud when, at the early age of forty-one, she died. It would have excited in her an amused incredulity, no doubt, had any one predicted that two generations after her death the real recognition of her powers was to come. Time, which like desert sands has effaced the footprints of so many promising authors, has, with her, served as the desert wind, to blow aside those dusts of the commonplace which for a while concealed her true proportions. She is loved more than she ever hoped to be, and far more widely known. Mrs. Ritchie tells somewhere an anecdote of a party of seven assembled at a dinner-table, where the question arose of the locality of one of Miss Austen's places,—Maple Grove, the residence of Mr. Suckling, if we are not mistaken,—and six of the persons present at once recognized the allusion, and had a formed opinion on the subject. The seventh was a Frenchman who did not read English!

Scott, Macaulay, Sir James Mackintosh, Miss Martineau, Mrs. Ritchie, Miss Mitford, and a host of others have vied in their generous tributes of admiration. But most striking of all, to our thinking, is that paid to Miss Austen by Lord Tennyson when, in some visit to Lyme not many years since, those with him pointed out this and the other feature of the place only to be interrupted with—"Never mind all that. Show me the exact spot where Louisa Musgrove fell!" Could non-historical verisimilitude go farther or mean more?

S. C. W.

NEWPORT, June, 1892.

LETTERS OF JANE AUSTEN

I.

STEVENTON, Thursday (January 16, 1796).

I HAVE just received yours and Mary's letter, and I thank you both, though their contents might have been more agreeable. I do not at all expect to see you on Tuesday, since matters have fallen out so unpleasantly; and if you are not able to return till after that day, it will hardly be possible for us to send for you before Saturday, though for my own part I care so little about the ball that it would be no sacrifice to me to give it up for the sake of seeing you two days earlier. We are extremely sorry for poor Eliza's illness. I trust, however, that she has continued to recover since you wrote, and that you will none of you be the worse for your attendance on her. What a good-for-nothing fellow Charles is to bespeak the stockings! I hope he will be too hot all the rest of his life for it!

I sent you a letter yesterday to Ibthorp, which I suppose you will not receive at Kintbury. It was not very long or very witty, and therefore if you never receive it, it does not much signify. I wrote principally to tell you that the Coopers were arrived and in good health. The little boy is very like Dr. Cooper, and the little girl is to resemble Jane, they say.

Our party to Ashe to-morrow night will consist of Edward Cooper, James (for a ball is nothing without him), Buller, who is now staying with us, and I. I look forward with great impatience to it, as I rather expect to receive an offer from my friend in the course of the evening. I shall refuse him, however, unless he promises to give away his white coat.

I am very much flattered by your commendation of my last letter, for I write only for fame, and without any view to pecuniary emolument.

Edward is gone to spend the day with his friend, John Lyford, and does not return till to-morrow. Anna is now here; she came up in her chaise to spend the day with her young cousins, but she does not much take to them or to anything about them, except Caroline's spinning-wheel. I am very glad to find from Mary that Mr. and Mrs. Fowle are pleased with you. I hope you will continue to give satisfaction.

How impertinent you are to write to me about Tom, as if I had not opportunities of hearing from him myself! The last letter that I received from him was dated on Friday, 8th, and he told me that if the wind should be favorable on Sunday, which it proved to be, they were to sail from Falmouth on that day. By this time, therefore, they are at Barbadoes, I suppose. The Rivers are still at Manydown, and are to be at Ashe to-morrow. I intended to call on the Miss Biggs yesterday had the weather been tolerable. Caroline, Anna, and I have just been devouring some cold souse, and it would be difficult to say which enjoyed it most.

Tell Mary that I make over Mr. Heartley and all his estate to her for her sole use and benefit in future, and not only him, but all my other admirers into the bargain wherever she can find them, even the kiss which C. Powlett wanted to give me, as I mean to confine myself in future to Mr. Tom Lefroy, for whom I don't care sixpence. Assure her also, as a last and indubitable proof of Warren's indifference to me, that he actually drew that gentleman's picture for me, and delivered it to me without a sigh.

Friday.—At length the day is come on which I am to flirt my last with Tom Lefroy, and when you receive this it will be over. My tears flow as I write at the melancholy idea. Wm. Chute called here yesterday. I wonder what he means by being so civil. There is a report that Tom is going to be married to a Lichfield lass. John Lyford and his sister bring Edward home to-day, dine with us, and we shall all go together to Ashe. I understand that we are to draw for partners. I shall be extremely impatient to hear from you again, that I may know how Eliza is, and when you are to return.

With best love, etc., I am affectionately yours,

J. AUSTEN.

Miss AUSTEN,
The Rev. Mr. Fowle's, Kintbury, Newbury

II.

CORK STREET, Tuesday morn (August, 1796).

MY DEAR CASSANDRA,—Here I am once more in this scene of dissipation and vice, and I begin already to find my morals corrupted. We reached Staines yesterday, I do not (know) when, without suffering so much from the heat as I had hoped to do. We set off again this morning at seven o'clock, and had a very pleasant drive, as the morning was cloudy and perfectly cool. I came all the way in the chaise from Hertford Bridge.

Edward[1] and Frank[2] are both gone out to seek their fortunes; the latter is to return soon and help us seek ours. The former we shall never see again. We are to be at Astley's to-night, which I am glad of. Edward has heard from Henry this morning. He has not been at the races at all, unless his driving Miss Pearson over to Rowling one day can be so called. We shall find him there on Thursday.

I hope you are all alive after our melancholy parting yesterday, and that you pursued your intended avocation with success. God bless you! I must leave off, for we are going out.

Yours very affectionately,
J. AUSTEN.

Everybody's love.

FOOTNOTES:

[1] Miss Austen's second brother.

[2] Francis, afterward Sir Francis Austen, Senior Admiral of the Fleet, and K. C. B.

III.

ROWLING, Monday (September 5).

MY DEAR CASSANDRA,—I shall be extremely anxious to hear the event of your ball, and shall hope to receive so long and minute an account of every particular that I shall be tired of reading it. Let me know how many, besides their fourteen selves and Mr. and Mrs. Wright, Michael will contrive to place about their coach, and how many of the gentlemen, musicians, and waiters he will have persuaded to come in their shooting-jackets. I hope John Lovett's accident will not prevent his attending the ball, as you will otherwise be obliged to dance with Mr. Tincton the whole evening. Let me know how J. Harwood deports himself without the Miss Biggs, and which of the Marys will carry the day with my brother James.

We were at a ball on Saturday, I assure you. We dined at Goodnestone, and in the evening danced two country-dances and the Boulangeries. I opened the ball with Edward Bridges; the other couples were Lewis Cage and Harriet, Frank and Louisa, Fanny and George. Elizabeth played one country-dance, Lady Bridges the other, which she made Henry dance with her, and Miss Finch played the Boulangeries.

In reading over the last three or four lines, I am aware of my having expressed myself in so doubtful a manner that if I did not tell you to the contrary, you might imagine it was Lady Bridges who made Henry dance with her at the same time that she was playing, which, if not impossible, must appear a very improbable event to you. But it was Elizabeth who danced. We supped there, and walked home at night under the shade of two umbrellas.

To-day the Goodnestone party begins to disperse and spread itself abroad. Mr. and Mrs. Cage and George repair to Hythe. Lady Waltham, Miss Bridges, and Miss Mary Finch to Dover, for the health of the two former. I have never seen Marianne at all. On Thursday Mr. and Mrs. Bridges return to Danbury; Miss Harriet Hales accompanies them to London on her way to Dorsetshire.

Farmer Claringbould died this morning, and I fancy Edward means to get some of his farm, if he can cheat Sir Brook enough in the agreement.

We have just got some venison from Godmersham, which the two Mr. Harveys are to dine on to-morrow, and on Friday or Saturday the Goodnestone people are to finish their scraps. Henry went away on Friday, as he purposed, *without fayl*. You will hear from him soon, I imagine, as he talked of writing to Steventon shortly. Mr. Richard Harvey is going to be married; but as it is a great secret, and only known to half the neighborhood, you must not mention it. The lady's name is Musgrave.

I am in great distress. I cannot determine whether I shall give Richis half a guinea or only five shillings when I go away. Counsel me, amiable Miss Austen, and tell me which will be the most.

We walked Frank last night to Crixhall Ruff, and he appeared much edified. Little Edward was breeched yesterday for good and all, and was whipped into the bargain.

Pray remember me to everybody who does not inquire after me; those who do, remember me without bidding. Give my love to Mary Harrison, and tell her I wish, whenever she is attached to a young man, some respectable Dr. Marchmont may keep them apart for five volumes....

IV.

ROWLING, Thursday (September 15).

MY DEAR CASSANDRA,—We have been very gay since I wrote last; dining at Nackington, returning by moonlight, and everything quite in style, not to mention Mr. Claringbould's funeral which we saw go by on Sunday. I believe I told you in a former letter that Edward had some idea of taking the name of Claringbould; but that scheme is over, though it would be a very eligible as well as a very pleasant plan, would any one advance him money enough to begin on. We rather expected Mr. Milles to have done so on Tuesday; but to our great surprise nothing was said on the subject, and unless it is in your power to assist your brother with five or six hundred pounds, he must entirely give up the idea.

At Nackington we met Lady Sondes' picture over the mantelpiece in the dining-room, and the pictures of her three children in an ante-room, besides Mr. Scott, Miss Fletcher, Mr. Toke, Mr. J. Toke, and the archdeacon Lynch. Miss Fletcher and I were very thick, but I am the thinnest of the two. She wore her purple muslin, which is pretty enough, though it does not become her complexion. There are two traits in her character which are pleasing,—namely, she admires Camilla, and drinks no cream in her tea. If you should ever see Lucy, you may tell her that I scolded Miss Fletcher for her negligence in writing, as she desired me to do, but without being able to bring her to any proper sense of shame,—that Miss Fletcher says, in her defence, that as everybody whom Lucy knew when she was in Canterbury has now left it, she has nothing at all to write to her about. By *everybody*, I suppose Miss Fletcher means that a new set of officers have arrived there. But this is a note of my own.

Mrs. Milles, Mr. John Toke, and in short everybody of any sensibility inquired in tender strains after you, and I took an opportunity of assuring Mr. J. T. that neither he nor his father need longer keep themselves single for you.

We went in our two carriages to Nackington; but how we divided I shall leave you to surmise, merely observing that as Elizabeth and I were without either hat or bonnet, it would not have been very convenient for us to go in the chaise. We went by Bifrons, and I contemplated with a melancholy pleasure the abode of him on whom I once fondly doated. We dine to-day at Goodnestone, to meet my aunt Fielding from Margate and a Mr. Clayton, her professed admirer—at least, so I imagine. Lady Bridges has received very good accounts of Marianne, who is already certainly the better for her bathing.

So His Royal Highness Sir Thomas Williams has at length sailed; the papers say "on a cruise." But I hope they are gone to Cork, or I shall have written in vain. Give my love to Jane, as she arrived at Steventon yesterday, I dare say.

I sent a message to Mr. Digweed from Edward in a letter to Mary Lloyd which she ought to receive to-day; but as I know that the Harwoods are not very exact as to their letters, I may as well repeat it to you. Mr. Digweed is to be informed that illness has prevented Seward's coming over to look at the repairs intended at the farm, but that he will come as soon as he can. Mr. Digweed may also be informed, if you think proper, that Mr. and Mrs. Milles are to dine here to-morrow, and that Mrs. Joan Knatchbull is to be asked to meet them. Mr. Richard Harvey's match is put off till he has got a better Christian name, of which he has great hopes.

Mr. Children's two sons are both going to be married, John and George. They are to have one wife between them, a Miss Holwell, who belongs to the Black Hole at Calcutta. I depend on hearing from James very soon; he promised me an account of the ball, and by this time he must have collected his ideas enough after the fatigue of dancing to give me one.

Edward and Fly went out yesterday very early in a couple of shooting jackets, and came home like a couple of bad shots, for they killed nothing at all. They are out again to-day, and are not yet returned. Delightful sport! They are just come home, Edward with his two brace, Frank with his two and a half. What amiable young men!

Friday.—Your letter and one from Henry are just come, and the contents of both accord with my scheme more than I had dared expect. In one particular I could wish it otherwise, for Henry is very indifferent indeed. You must not expect us quite so early, however, as Wednesday, the 20th,—on that day se'nnight, according to our present plan, we may be with you. Frank had never any idea of going away before Monday, the 26th. I shall write to Miss Mason immediately, and press her returning with us, which Henry thinks very likely, and particularly eligible.

Buy Mary Harrison's gown by all means. You shall have mine for ever so much money, though, if I am tolerably rich when I get home, I shall like it very much myself.

As to the mode of our travelling to town, *I* want to go in a stage-coach, but Frank will not let me. As you are likely to have the Williams and Lloyds with you next week, you would hardly find room for us then. If any one wants anything in town, they must send their commissions to Frank, as *I* shall merely pass through it. The tallow-chandler is Penlington, at the Crown and Beehive, Charles Street, Covent Garden.

Miss AUSTEN, Steventon, Overton, Hants.

V.

ROWLING, Sunday (September 18).

MY DEAR CASSANDRA,—This morning has been spent in doubt and deliberation, in forming plans and removing difficulties, for it ushered in the day with an event which I had not intended should take place so soon by a week. Frank has received his appointment on board the "Captain John Gore," commanded by the "Triton," and will therefore be obliged to be in town on Wednesday; and though I have every disposition in the world to accompany him on that day, I cannot go on the uncertainty of the Pearsons being at home, as I should not have a place to go to in case they were from home.

I wrote to Miss P. on Friday, and hoped to receive an answer from her this morning, which would have rendered everything smooth and easy, and would have enabled us to leave this place to-morrow, as Frank, on first receiving his appointment, intended to do. He remains till Wednesday merely to accommodate me. I have written to her again to-day, and desired her to answer it by return of post. On Tuesday, therefore, I shall positively know whether they can receive me on Wednesday. If they cannot, Edward has been so good as to promise to take me to Greenwich on the Monday following, which was the day before fixed on, if that suits them better. If I have no answer at all on Tuesday, I must suppose Mary is not at home, and must wait till I do hear, as after having invited her to go to Steventon with me, it will not quite do to go home and say no more about it.

My father will be so good as to fetch home his prodigal daughter from town, I hope, unless he wishes me to walk the hospitals, enter at the Temple, or mount guard at St. James'. It will hardly be in Frank's power to take me home,—nay, it certainly will not. I shall write again as soon as I get to Greenwich.

What dreadful hot weather we have! It keeps one in a continual state of inelegance.

If Miss Pearson should return with me, pray be careful not to expect too much beauty. I will not pretend to say that on a first view she quite answered the opinion I had formed of her. My mother, I am sure, will be disappointed if she does not take great care. From what I remember of her picture, it is no great resemblance.

I am very glad that the idea of returning with Frank occurred to me; for as to Henry's coming into Kent again, the time of its taking place is so very uncertain that I should be waiting for dead men's shoes. I had once determined to go with Frank to-morrow and take my chance, etc., but they dissuaded me from so rash a step as I really think on consideration it would have been; for if the Pearsons were not at home, I should inevitably fall a sacrifice to the arts of some fat woman who would make me drunk with small beer.

Mary is brought to bed of a boy,—both doing very well. I shall leave you to guess what Mary I mean. Adieu, with best love to all your agreeable inmates. Don't let the Lloyds go on any account before I return, unless Miss P. is of the party. How ill I have written! I begin to hate myself.

Yours ever,
J. AUSTEN.

The "Triton" is a new 32 frigate just launched at Deptford. Frank is much pleased with the prospect of having Captain Gore under his command.

Miss AUSTEN, Steventon, Overton, Hants.

VI.

"BULL AND GEORGE," DARTFORD,
Wednesday (October 24, 1798).

MY DEAR CASSANDRA,—You have already heard from Daniel, I conclude, in what excellent time we reached and quitted Sittingbourne, and how very well my mother bore her journey thither. I am now able to send you a continuation of the same good account of her. She was very little fatigued on her arrival at this place, has been refreshed by a comfortable dinner, and now seems quite stout. It wanted five minutes of twelve when we left Sittingbourne, from whence we had a famous pair of horses, which took us to Rochester in an hour and a quarter; the postboy seemed determined to show my mother that Kentish drivers were not always tedious, and really drove as fast as Cax.

Our next stage was not quite so expeditiously performed; the road was heavy, and our horses very indifferent. However, we were in such good time and my mother bore her journey so well, that expedition was of little importance to us; and as it was, we were very little more than two hours and a half coming hither, and it was scarcely past four when we stopped at the inn. My mother took some of her bitters at Osprönge, and some more at Rochester, and she ate some bread several times.

We have got apartments up two pair of stairs, as we could not be otherwise accommodated with a sitting-room and bed-chambers on the same floor which we wished to be. We have one double-bedded and one single-bedded room; in the former my mother and I are to sleep. I shall leave you to guess who is to occupy the other. We sate down to dinner a little after five, and had some beef-steaks and a boiled fowl, but no oyster sauce.

I should have begun my letter soon after our arrival, but for a little adventure which prevented me. After we had been here a quarter of an hour it was discovered that my writing and dressing boxes had been by accident put into a chaise which was just packing off as we came in, and were driven away toward Gravesend in their way to the West Indies. No part of my property could have been such a prize before, for in my writing-box was all my worldly wealth, 7*l.*, and my dear Harry's deputation. Mr. Nottley immediately despatched a man and horse after the chaise, and in half an hour's time I had the pleasure of being as rich as ever; they were got about two or three miles off.

My day's journey has been pleasanter in every respect than I expected. I have been very little crowded and by no means unhappy. Your watchfulness with regard to the weather on our accounts was very kind and very effectual. We had one heavy shower on leaving Sittingbourne, but afterwards the clouds cleared away, and we had a very bright *chrystal* afternoon.

My father is now reading the "Midnight Bell," which he has got from the library, and mother sitting by the fire. Our route to-morrow is not determined. We have none of us much inclination for London, and if Mr. Nottley will give us leave, I think we shall go to Staines through Croydon and Kingston, which will be much pleasanter than any other way; but he is decidedly for Clapham and Battersea. God bless you all!

Yours affectionately, J. A.

I flatter myself that *itty Dordy* will not forget me at least under a week. Kiss him for me.

Miss AUSTEN,
Godmersham Park, Faversham.

VII.

STEVENTON, Saturday (October 27).

MY DEAR CASSANDRA,—Your letter was a most agreeable surprise to me to-day, and I have taken a long sheet of paper to show my gratitude.

We arrived here yesterday between four and five, but I cannot send you quite so triumphant an account of our last day's journey as of the first and second. Soon after I had finished my letter from Staines, my mother began to suffer from the exercise or fatigue of travelling, and she was a good deal indisposed. She had not a very good night at Staines, but bore her journey better than I had expected, and at Basingstoke, where we stopped more than half an hour, received much comfort from a mess of broth and the sight of Mr. Lyford, who recommended her to take twelve drops of laudanum when she went to bed as a composer, which she accordingly did.

James called on us just as we were going to tea, and my mother was well enough to talk very cheerfully to him before she went to bed. James seems to have taken to his old trick of coming to Steventon in spite of Mary's reproaches, for he was here before breakfast and is now paying us a second visit. They were to have dined here to-day, but the weather is too bad. I have had the pleasure of hearing that Martha is with them. James fetched her from Ibthorp on Thursday, and she will stay with them till she removes to Kintbury.

We met with no adventures at all in our journey yesterday, except that our trunk had once nearly slipped off, and we were obliged to stop at Hartley to have our wheels greased.

Whilst my mother and Mr. Lyford were together I went to Mrs. Ryder's and bought what I intended to buy, but not in much perfection. There were no narrow braces for children, and scarcely any notting silk; but Miss Wood, as usual, is going to town very soon, and will lay in a fresh stock. I gave 2s. 3d. a yard for my flannel, and I fancy it is not very good, but it is so disgraceful and contemptible an article in itself that its being comparatively good or bad is of little importance. I bought some Japan ink likewise, and next week shall begin my operations on my hat, on which you know my principal hopes of happiness depend.

I am very grand indeed; I had the dignity of dropping out my mother's laudanum last night. I carry about the keys of the wine and closet, and twice since I began this letter have had orders to give in the kitchen. Our dinner was very good yesterday, and the chicken boiled perfectly tender; therefore I shall not be obliged to dismiss Nanny on that account.

Almost everything was unpacked and put away last night. Nanny chose to do it, and I was not sorry to be busy. I have unpacked the gloves, and placed yours in your drawer. Their color is light and pretty, and I believe exactly what we fixed on.

Your letter was chaperoned here by one from Mrs. Cooke, in which she says that "Battleridge" is not to come out before January, and she is so little satisfied with Cawthorn's dilatoriness that she never means to employ him again.

Mrs. Hall, of Sherborne, was brought to bed yesterday of a dead child, some weeks before she expected, owing to a fright. I suppose she happened unawares to look at her husband.

There has been a great deal of rain here for this last fortnight, much more than in Kent, and indeed we found the roads all the way from Staines most disgracefully dirty. Steventon lane has its full share of it, and I don't know when I shall be able to get to Deane.

I hear that Martha is in better looks and spirits than she has enjoyed for a long time, and I flatter myself she will now be able to jest openly about Mr. W.

The spectacles which Molly found are my mother's, the scissors my father's. We are very glad to hear such a good account of your patients, little and great. My dear itty Dordy's remembrance of me is very pleasing to me,—foolishly pleasing, because I know it will be over so soon. My attachment to him will be more durable. I shall think with tenderness and delight on his beautiful and smiling countenance and interesting manner until a few years have turned him into an ungovernable, ungracious fellow.

The books from Winton are all unpacked and put away; the binding has compressed them most conveniently, and there is now very good room in the bookcase for all that we wish to have there. I believe the servants were very glad to see us Nanny was, I am sure. She confesses that it was very dull, and yet she had her child with her till last Sunday. I understand that there are some grapes left, but I believe not many; they must be gathered as soon as possible, or this rain will entirely rot them.

I am quite angry with myself for not writing closer; why is my alphabet so much more sprawly than yours? Dame Tilbury's daughter has lain in. Shall I give her any of your baby clothes? The laceman was here only a few days ago. How unfortunate for both of us that he came so soon! Dame Bushell washes for us only one week more, as Sukey has got a place. John Steevens' wife undertakes our purification. She does not look as if anything she touched would ever be clean, but who knows? We do not seem likely to have any other maidservant at present, but Dame Staples will supply the place of one. Mary has hired a young girl from Ashe who has never been out to service to be her scrub, but James fears her not being strong enough for the place.

Earle Harwood has been to Deane lately, as I think Mary wrote us word, and his family then told him that they would receive his wife, if she continued to behave well for another year. He was very grateful, as well he might; their behavior throughout the whole affair has been particularly kind. Earle and his wife live in the most private manner imaginable at Portsmouth, without keeping a servant of any kind. What a prodigious innate love of virtue she must have, to marry under such circumstances!

It is now Saturday evening, but I wrote the chief of this in the morning. My mother has not been down at all to-day; the laudanum made her sleep a good deal, and upon the whole I think she is better. My father and I dined by ourselves. How strange! He and John Bond are now very happy together, for I have just heard the heavy step of the latter along the passage.

James Digweed called to-day, and I gave him his brother's deputation. Charles Harwood, too, has just called to ask how we are, in his way from Dummer, whither he has been conveying Miss Garrett, who is going to return to her former residence in Kent. I will leave off, or I shall not have room to add a word to-morrow.

Sunday.—My mother has had a very good night, and feels much better to-day.

I have received my aunt's letter, and thank you for your scrap. I will write to Charles soon. Pray give Fanny and Edward a kiss from me, and ask George if he has got a new song for me. 'Tis really very kind of my aunt to ask us to Bath again; a kindness that deserves a better return than to profit by it.

Yours ever,   J. A.

Miss AUSTEN,
Godmersham Park, Faversham, Kent.

VIII.

STEVENTON, December 1.

MY DEAR CASSANDRA,—I am so good as to write to you again thus speedily, to let you know that I have just heard from Frank. He was at Cadiz, alive and well, on October 19, and had then very lately received a letter from you, written as long ago as when the "London" was at St. Helen's. But his *raly* latest intelligence of us was in one from me of September 1, which I sent soon after we got to Godmersham. He had written a packet full for his dearest friends in England, early in October, to go by the "Excellent;" but the "Excellent" was not sailed, nor likely to sail, when he despatched this to me. It comprehended letters for both of us, for Lord Spencer, Mr. Daysh, and the East India Directors. Lord St. Vincent had left the fleet when he wrote, and was gone to Gibraltar, it was said to superintend the fitting out of a private expedition from thence against some of the enemies' ports; Minorca or Malta were conjectured to be the objects.

Frank writes in good spirits, but says that our correspondence cannot be so easily carried on in future as it has been, as the communication between Cadiz and Lisbon is less frequent than formerly. You and my mother, therefore, must not alarm yourselves at the long intervals that may divide his letters. I address this advice to you two as being the most tender-hearted of the family.

My mother made her *entrée* into the dressing-room through crowds of admiring spectators yesterday afternoon, and we all drank tea together for the first time these five weeks. She has had a tolerable night, and bids fair for a continuance in the same brilliant course of action to-day....

Mr. Lyford was here yesterday; he came while we were at dinner, and partook of our elegant entertainment. I was not ashamed at asking him to sit down to table, for we had some pease-soup, a sparerib, and a pudding. He wants my mother to look yellow and to throw out a rash, but she will do neither.

I was at Deane yesterday morning. Mary was very well, but does not gain bodily strength very fast. When I saw her so stout on the third and sixth days, I expected to have seen her as well as ever by the end of a fortnight.

James went to Ibthorp yesterday to see his mother and child. Letty is with Mary[3] at present, of course exceedingly happy, and in raptures with the child. Mary does not manage matters in such a way as to make me want to lay in myself. She is not tidy enough in her appearance; she has no dressing-gown to sit up in; her curtains are all too thin, and things are not in that comfort and style about her which are necessary to make such a situation an enviable one. Elizabeth was really a pretty object with her nice clean cap put on so tidily and her dress so uniformly white and orderly. We live entirely in the dressing-room now, which I like very much; I always feel so much more elegant in it than in the parlor.

No news from Kintbury yet. Eliza sports with our impatience. She was very well last Thursday. Who is Miss Maria Montresor going to marry, and what is to become of Miss Mulcaster?

I find great comfort in my stuff gown, but I hope you do not wear yours too often. I have made myself two or three caps to wear of evenings since I came home, and they save me a world of torment as to hairdressing, which at present gives me no trouble beyond washing and brushing, for my long hair is always plaited up out of sight, and my short hair curls well enough to want no papering. I have had it cut lately by Mr. Butler.

There is no reason to suppose that Miss Morgan is dead after all. Mr. Lyford gratified us very much yesterday by his praises of my father's mutton, which they all think the finest that was ever ate. John Bond begins to find himself grow old, which John Bonds ought not to do, and unequal to much hard work; a man is therefore hired to supply his place as to labor, and John himself is to have the care of the sheep. There are not more people engaged than before, I believe; only men instead of boys. I fancy so at least, but you know my stupidity as to such matters. Lizzie Bond is just apprenticed to Miss Small, so we may hope to see her able to spoil gowns in a few years.

My father has applied to Mr. May for an ale-house for Robert, at his request, and to Mr. Deane, of Winchester, likewise. This was my mother's idea, who thought he would be proud to oblige a relation of Edward in return for Edward's accepting his money. He sent a very civil answer indeed, but has no house vacant at present. May expects to have an empty one soon at Farnham, so perhaps Nanny may have the honor of drawing ale for the Bishop. I shall write to Frank to-morrow.

Charles Powlett gave a dance on Thursday, to the great disturbance of all his neighbors, of course, who, you know, take a most lively interest in the state of his finances, and live in hopes of his being soon ruined.

We are very much disposed to like our new maid; she knows nothing of a dairy, to be sure, which, in our family, is rather against her, but she is to be taught it all. In short, we have felt the inconvenience of being without a maid so long, that we are determined to like her, and she will find it a hard matter to displease us. As yet, she seems to cook very well, is uncommonly stout, and says she can work well at her needle.

Sunday.—My father is glad to hear so good an account of Edward's pigs, and desires he may be told, as encouragement to his taste for them, that Lord Bolton is particularly curious in *his* pigs, has had pigstyes of a most elegant construction built for them, and visits them every morning as soon as he rises.

Affectionately yours,
J. A.

Miss AUSTEN,
Godmersham Park, Faversham.

FOOTNOTE:

[3] Mrs. James Austen.

IX.

STEVENTON, Tuesday (December 18).

MY DEAR CASSANDRA,—Your letter came quite as soon as I expected, and so your letters will always do, because I have made it a rule not to expect them till they come, in which I think I consult the ease of us both.

It is a great satisfaction to us to hear that your business is in a way to be settled, and so settled as to give you as little inconvenience as possible. You are very welcome to my father's name and to his services if they are ever required in it. I shall keep my ten pounds too, to wrap myself up in next winter.

I took the liberty a few days ago of asking your black velvet bonnet to lend me its cawl, which it very readily did, and by which I have been enabled to give a considerable improvement of dignity to cap, which was before too *nidgetty* to please me. I shall wear it on Thursday, but I hope you will not be offended with me for following your advice as to its ornaments only in part. I still venture to retain the narrow silver round it, put twice round without any bow, and instead of the black military feather shall put in the coquelicot one as being smarter, and besides coquelicot is to be all the fashion this winter. After the ball I shall probably make it entirely black.

I am sorry that our dear Charles begins to feel the dignity of ill-usage. My father will write to Admiral Gambier. He must have already received so much satisfaction from his acquaintance and patronage of Frank, that he will be delighted, I dare say, to have another of the family introduced to him. I think it would be very right in Charles to address Sir Thomas on the occasion, though

I cannot approve of your scheme of writing to him (which you communicated to me a few nights ago) to request him to come home and convey you to Steventon. To do you justice, however, you had some doubts of the propriety of such a measure yourself.

I am very much obliged to my dear little George for his message,—for his love at least; his duty, I suppose, was only in consequence of some hint of my favorable intentions towards him from his father or mother. I am sincerely rejoiced, however, that I ever was born, since it has been the means of procuring him a dish of tea. Give my best love to him....

Wednesday.—I have changed my mind, and changed the trimmings of my cap this morning; they are now such as you suggested. I felt as if I should not prosper if I strayed from your directions, and I think it makes me look more like Lady Conyngham now than it did before, which is all that one lives for now. I believe I *shall* make my new gown like my robe, but the back of the latter is all in a piece with the tail, and will seven yards enable me to copy it in that respect? . . .

I have just heard from Martha and Frank: his letter was written on November 12. All well and nothing particular.

J. A.

Miss AUSTEN,
Godmersham Park, Faversham.

X.

STEVENTON, Monday night (December 24).

MY DEAR CASSANDRA,—I have got some pleasant news for you which I am eager to communicate, and therefore begin my letter sooner, though I shall not send it sooner than usual.

Admiral Gambier, in reply to my father's application, writes as follows: "As it is usual to keep young officers in small vessels, it being most proper on account of their inexperience, and it being also a situation where they are more in the way of learning their duty, your son has been continued in the 'Scorpion;' but I have mentioned to the Board of Admiralty his wish to be in a frigate, and when a proper opportunity offers and it is judged that he has taken his turn in a small ship, I hope he will be removed. With regard to your son now in the 'London' I am glad I can give you the assurance that his promotion is likely to take place very soon, as Lord Spencer has been so good as to say he would include him in an arrangement that he proposes making in a short time relative to some promotions in that quarter."

There! I may now finish my letter and go and hang myself, for I am sure I can neither write nor do anything which will not appear insipid to you after this. *Now* I really think he will soon be made, and only wish we could communicate our foreknowledge of the event to him whom it principally concerns. My father has written to Daysh to desire that he will inform us, if he can, when the commission is sent. Your chief wish is now ready to be accomplished; and could Lord Spencer give happiness to Martha at the same time, what a joyful heart he would make of yours!

I have sent the same extract of the sweets of Gambier to Charles, who, poor fellow, though he sinks into nothing but an humble attendant on the hero of the piece, will, I hope, be contented with the prospect held out to him. By what the Admiral says, it appears as if he had been designedly kept in the "Scorpion." But I will not torment myself with conjectures and suppositions; facts shall satisfy me.

Frank had not heard from any of us for ten weeks when he wrote to me on November 12 in consequence of Lord St. Vincent being removed to Gibraltar. When his commission is sent, however, it will not be so long on its road as our letters, because all the Government despatches are forwarded by land to his lordship from Lisbon with great regularity.

I returned from Manydown this morning, and found my mother certainly in no respect worse than when I left her. She does not like the cold weather, but that we cannot help. I spent my time very quietly and very pleasantly with Catherine. Miss Blackford is agreeable enough. I do not want people to be very agreeable, as it saves me the trouble of liking them a great deal. I found only Catherine and her when I got to Manydown on Thursday. We dined together, and went together to Worting to seek the protection of Mrs. Clarke, with whom were Lady Mildmay, her eldest son, and Mr. and Mrs. Hoare.

Our ball was very thin, but by no means unpleasant. There were thirty-one people, and only eleven ladies out of the number, and but five single women in the room. Of the gentlemen present you may have some idea from the list of my partners,—Mr. Wood, G. Lefroy, Rice, a Mr. Butcher (belonging to the Temples, a sailor and not of the 11th Light Dragoons), Mr. Temple (not the horrid one of all), Mr. Wm. Orde (cousin to the Kingsclere man), Mr. John Harwood, and Mr. Calland, who appeared as usual with his hat in his hand, and stood every now and then behind Catherine and me to be talked to and abused for not dancing. We teased him, however, into it at last. I was very glad to see him again after so long a separation, and he was altogether rather the genius and flirt of the evening. He inquired after you.

There were twenty dances, and I danced them all, and without any fatigue. I was glad to find myself capable of dancing so much, and with so much satisfaction as I did; from my slender enjoyment of the Ashford balls (as assemblies for dancing) I had not thought myself equal to it, but in cold weather and with few couples I fancy I could just as well dance for a week together as for half an hour. My black cap was openly admired by Mrs. Lefroy, and secretly I imagine by everybody else in the room....

Poor Edward! It is very hard that he, who has everything else in the world that he can wish for, should not have good health too. But I hope with the assistance of stomach complaints, faintnesses, and sicknesses, he will soon be restored to that blessing likewise. If his nervous complaint proceeded from a suppression of something that ought to be thrown out, which does not seem unlikely, the first of these disorders may really be a remedy, and I sincerely wish it may, for I know no one more deserving of happiness without alloy than Edward is....

The Lords of the Admiralty will have enough of our applications at present, for I hear from Charles that he has written to Lord Spencer himself to be removed. I am afraid his Serene Highness will be in a passion, and order some of our heads to be cut off....

You deserve a longer letter than this; but it is my unhappy fate seldom to treat people so well as they deserve.... God bless you!

Yours affectionately,
JANE AUSTEN.

Wednesday.—The snow came to nothing yesterday, so I did go to Deane, and returned home at nine o'clock at night in the little carriage, and without being very cold.

Miss AUSTEN,
Godmersham Park, Faversham, Kent.

XI.

STEVENTON, Friday (December 28).

MY DEAR CASSANDRA,—Frank is made. He was yesterday raised to the rank of Commander, and appointed to the "Petterel" sloop, now at Gibraltar. A letter from Daysh has just announced this, and as it is confirmed by a very friendly one from Mr. Mathew to the same effect, transcribing one from Admiral Gambier to the General, we have no reason to suspect the truth of it.

As soon as you have cried a little for joy, you may go on, and learn further that the India House have taken *Captain Austen's* petition into consideration,—this comes from Daysh,—and likewise that Lieutenant Charles John Austen is removed to the "Tamar" frigate,—this comes from the Admiral. We cannot find out where the "Tamar" is, but I hope we shall now see Charles here at all events.

This letter is to be dedicated entirely to good news. If you will send my father an account of your washing and letter expenses, etc., he will send you a draft for the amount of it, as well as for your next quarter, and for Edward's rent. If you don't buy a muslin gown now on the strength of this money and Frank's promotion, I shall never forgive you.

Mrs. Lefroy has just sent me word that Lady Dorchester meant to invite me to her ball on January 8, which, though an humble blessing compared with what the last page records, I do not consider as any calamity.

I cannot write any more now, but I have written enough to make you very happy, and therefore may safely conclude.

Yours affectionately,
JANE.

Miss AUSTEN, Godmersham Park.

XII.

STEVENTON, Tuesday (January 8, 1799).

MY DEAR CASSANDRA,—You must read your letters over *five* times in future before you send them, and then, perhaps, you may find them as entertaining as I do. I laughed at several parts of the one which I am now answering.

Charles is not come yet, but he must come this morning, or he shall never know what I will do to him. The ball at Kempshott is this evening, and I have got him an invitation, though I have not been so considerate as to get him a partner. But the cases are different between him and Eliza Bailey, for he is not in a dying way, and may therefore be equal to getting a partner for himself. I believe I told you that Monday was to be the ball night, for which, and for all other errors into which I may ever have led you, I humbly ask your pardon.

Elizabeth is very cruel about my writing music, and, as a punishment for her, I should insist upon always writing out all hers for her in future, if I were not punishing myself at the same time.

I am tolerably glad to hear that Edward's income is so good a one,—as glad as I can be at anybody's being rich except you and me,—and I am thoroughly rejoiced to hear of his present to you.

I am not to wear my white satin cap to-night, after all; I am to wear a mamalone cap instead, which Charles Fowle sent to Mary, and which she lends me. It is all the fashion now; worn at the opera, and by Lady Mildmays at Hackwood balls. I hate describing such things, and I dare say you will be able to guess what it is like. I have got over the dreadful epocha of mantua-making much better than I expected. My gown is made very much like my blue one, which you always told me sat very well, with only these variations: the sleeves are short, the wrap fuller, the apron comes over it, and a band of the same completes the whole.

I assure you that I dread the idea of going to Brighton as much as you do, but I am not without hopes that something may happen to prevent it.

F—— has lost his election at B——, and perhaps they may not be able to see company for some time. They talk of going to Bath, too, in the spring, and perhaps they may be overturned in their way down, and all laid up for the summer.

Wednesday.—I have had a cold and weakness in one of my eyes for some days, which makes writing neither very pleasant nor very profitable, and which will probably prevent my finishing this letter myself. My mother has undertaken to do it for me, and I shall leave the Kempshott ball for her.

You express so little anxiety about my being murdered under Ash Park Copse by Mrs. Hulbert's servant, that I have a great mind not to tell you whether I was or not, and shall only say that I did not return home that night or the next, as Martha kindly made room for me in her bed, which was the shut-up one in the new nursery. Nurse and the child slept upon the floor, and there we all were in some confusion and great comfort. The bed did exceedingly well for us, both to lie awake in and talk till two o'clock, and to sleep in the rest of the night. I love Martha better than ever, and I mean to go and see her, if I can, when she gets home. We all dined at the Harwoods' on Thursday, and the party broke up the next morning.

This complaint in my eye has been a sad bore to me, for I have not been able to read or work in any comfort since Friday; but one advantage will be derived from it, for I shall be such a proficient in music by the time I have got rid of my cold, that I shall be perfectly qualified in that science at least to take Mr. Roope's office at Eastwell next summer; and I am sure of Elizabeth's recommendation, be it only on Harriet's account. Of my talent in drawing I have given specimens in my letters to you, and I have nothing to do but to invent a few hard names for the stars.

Mary grows rather more reasonable about her child's beauty, and says that she does not think him really handsome; but I suspect her moderation to be something like that of W——W——'s mamma. Perhaps Mary has told you that they are going to enter more into dinner-parties; the Biggs and Mr. Holder dine there to-morrow, and I am to meet them. I shall sleep there. Catherine has the honor of giving her name to a set, which will be composed of two Withers, two Heathcotes, a Blackford, and no Bigg except herself. She congratulated me last night on Frank's promotion, as if she really felt the joy she talked of.

My sweet little George! I am delighted to hear that he has such an inventive genius as to face-making. I admired his yellow wafer very much, and hope he will choose the wafer for your next letter. I wore my green shoes last night, and took my white fan with me; I am very glad he never threw it into the river.

Mrs. Knight giving up the Godmersham estate to Edward was no such prodigious act of generosity after all, it seems, for she has reserved herself an income out of it still; this ought to be known, that her conduct may not be overrated. I rather think Edward shows the most magnanimity of the two, in accepting her resignation with such incumbrances.

The more I write, the better my eye gets; so I shall at least keep on till it is quite well, before I give up my pen to my mother.

Mrs. Bramston's little movable apartment was tolerably filled last night by herself, Mrs. H. Blackstone, her two daughters, and me. I do not like the Miss Blackstones; indeed, I was always determined not to like them, so there is the less merit in it. Mrs. Bramston was very civil, kind, and noisy. I spent a very pleasant evening, chiefly among the Manydown party. There was the same kind of supper as last year, and the same want of chairs. There were more dancers than the room could conveniently hold, which is enough to constitute a good ball at any time.

I do not think I was very much in request. People were rather apt not to ask me till they could not help it; one's consequence, you know, varies so much at times without any particular reason. There was one gentleman, an officer of the Cheshire, a very good-looking young man, who, I was told, wanted very much to be introduced to me; but as he did not want it quite enough to take much trouble in effecting it, we never could bring it about.

I danced with Mr. John Wood again, twice with a Mr. South, a lad from Winchester, who, I suppose, is as far from being related to the bishop of that diocese as it is possible to be, with G. Lefroy, and J. Harwood, who, I think, takes to me rather more than he used to do. One of my gayest actions was sitting down two dances in preference to having Lord Bolton's eldest son for my partner, who danced too ill to be endured. The Miss Charterises were there, and played the parts of the Miss Edens with great spirit. Charles never came. Naughty Charles! I suppose he could not get superseded in time.

Miss Debary has replaced your two sheets of drawing-paper with two of superior size and quality; so I do not grudge her having taken them at all now. Mr. Ludlow and Miss Pugh of Andover are lately married, and so is Mrs. Skeete of Basingstoke, and Mr. French, chemist, of Reading.

I do not wonder at your wanting to read "First Impressions" again, so seldom as you have gone through it, and that so long ago. I am much obliged to you for meaning to leave my old petticoat behind you. I have long secretly wished it might be done, but had not courage to make the request.

Pray mention the name of Maria Montresor's lover when you write next. My mother wants to know it, and I have not courage to look back into your letters to find it out.

I shall not be able to send this till to-morrow, and you will be disappointed on Friday; I am very sorry for it, but I cannot help it. The partnership between Jeffereys, Toomer, and Legge is dissolved; the two latter are melted away into nothing, and it is to be hoped that Jeffereys will soon break, for the sake of a few heroines whose money he may have. I wish you joy of your birthday twenty times over.

I shall be able to send this to the post to-day, which exalts me to the utmost pinnacle of human felicity, and makes me bask in the sunshine of prosperity or gives me any other sensation of pleasure in studied language which you may prefer. Do not be angry with me for not filling my sheet, and believe me yours affectionately,

J. A.

Miss AUSTEN,
Godmersham Park, Faversham.

XIII.

STEVENTON, Monday (January 21).

MY DEAR CASSANDRA,—I will endeavor to make this letter more worthy your acceptance than my last, which was so shabby a one that I think Mr. Marshall could never charge you with the postage. My eyes have been very indifferent since it was written, but are now getting better once more; keeping them so many hours open on Thursday night, as well as the dust of the ballroom, injured them a good deal. I use them as little as I can, but you know, and Elizabeth knows, and everybody who ever had weak eyes knows, how delightful it is to hurt them by employment, against the advice and entreaty of all one's friends.

Charles leaves us to-night. The "Tamar" is in the Downs, and Mr. Daysh advises him to join her there directly, as there is no chance of her going to the westward. Charles does not approve of this at all, and will not be much grieved if he should be too late for her before she sails, as he may then hope to get into a better station. He attempted to go to town last night, and got as far on his road thither as Dean Gate; but both the coaches were full, and we had the pleasure of seeing him back again. He will call on Daysh to-morrow to know whether the "Tamar" has sailed or not, and if she is still at the Downs he will proceed in one of the night coaches to Deal. I want to go with him, that I may explain the country to him properly between Canterbury and Rowling, but the unpleasantness of returning by myself deters me. I should like to go as far as Ospringe with him very much indeed, that I might surprise you at Godmersham.

Martha writes me word that Charles was very much admired at Kintbury, and Mrs. Lefroy never saw any one so much improved in her life, and thinks him handsomer than Henry. He appears to far more advantage here than he did at Godmersham, not surrounded by strangers and neither oppressed by a pain in his face or powder in his hair.

James christened Elizabeth Caroline on Saturday morning, and then came home. Mary, Anna, and Edward have left us of course; before the second went I took down her answer to her cousin Fanny.

Yesterday came a letter to my mother from Edward Cooper to announce, not the birth of a child, but of a living; for Mrs. Leigh has begged his acceptance of the Rectory of Hamstall-Ridware in Staffordshire, vacant by Mr. Johnson's death. We collect from his letter that he means to reside there, in which he shows his wisdom. Staffordshire is a good way off; so we shall see nothing more of them till, some fifteen years hence, the Miss Coopers are presented to us, fine, jolly, handsome, ignorant girls. The living is valued at 140*l*. a year, but perhaps it may be improvable. How will they be able to convey the furniture of the dressing-room so far in safety?

Our first cousins seem all dropping off very fast. One is incorporated into the family, another dies, and a third goes into Staffordshire. We can learn nothing of the disposal of the other living. I have not the smallest notion of Fulwar's having it. Lord Craven has probably other connections and more intimate ones, in that line, than he now has with the Kintbury family.

Our ball on Thursday was a very poor one, only eight couple and but twenty-three people in the room; but it was not the ball's fault, for we were deprived of two or three families by the sudden illness of Mr. Wither, who was seized that morning at Winchester with a return of his former alarming complaint. An express was sent off from thence to the family; Catherine and Miss Blackford were dining with Mrs. Russell. Poor Catherine's distress must have been very great. She was prevailed on to wait till the Heathcotes could come from Wintney, and then with those two and Harris proceeded directly to Winchester. In such a disorder his danger, I suppose, must always be great; but from this attack he is now rapidly recovering, and will be well enough to return to Manydown, I fancy, in a few days.

It was a fine thing for conversation at the ball. But it deprived us not only of the Biggs, but of Mrs. Russell too, and of the Boltons and John Harwood, who were dining there likewise, and of Mr. Lane, who kept away as related to the family. Poor man!—I mean Mr. Wither—his life is so useful, his character so respectable and worthy, that I really believe there was a good deal of sincerity in the general concern expressed on his account.

Our ball was chiefly made up of Jervoises and Terrys, the former of whom were apt to be vulgar, the latter to be noisy. I had an odd set of partners: Mr. Jenkins, Mr. Street, Colonel Jervoise, James Digweed, J. Lyford, and Mr. Briggs, a friend of the latter. I had a very pleasant evening, however, though you will probably find out that there was no particular reason for it; but I do not think it worth while to wait for enjoyment until there is some real opportunity for it. Mary behaved very well, and was not at all fidgetty. For the history of her adventures at the ball I refer you to Anna's letter.

When you come home you will have some shirts to make up for Charles. Mrs. Davies frightened him into buying a piece of Irish when we were in Basingstoke. Mr. Daysh supposes that Captain Austen's commission has reached him by this time.

Tuesday.—Your letter has pleased and amused me very much. Your essay on happy fortnights is highly ingenious, and the talobert skin made me laugh a good deal. Whenever I fall into misfortune, how many jokes it ought to furnish to my acquaintance in general, or I shall die dreadfully in their debt for entertainment.

It began to occur to me before you mentioned it that I had been somewhat silent as to my mother's health for some time, but I thought you could have no difficulty in divining its exact state,—you, who have guessed so much stranger things. She is tolerably well,—better upon the whole than she was some weeks ago. She would tell you herself that she has a very dreadful cold in her head at present; but I have not much compassion for colds in the head without fever or sore throat.

Our own particular little brother got a place in the coach last night, and is now, I suppose, in town. I have no objection at all to your buying our gowns there, as your imagination has pictured to you exactly such a one as is necessary to make me happy. You quite abash me by your progress in notting, for I am still without silk. You must get me some in town or in Canterbury; it should be finer than yours.

I thought Edward would not approve of Charles being a crop, and rather wished you to conceal it from him at present, lest it might fall on his spirits and retard his recovery. My father furnishes him with a pig from Cheesedown; it is already killed and cut up, but it is not to weigh more than nine stone; the season is too far advanced to get him a larger one. My mother means to pay herself for the salt and the trouble of ordering it to be cured by the spareribs, the souse, and the lard. We have had one dead lamb.

I congratulate you on Mr. E. Hatton's good fortune. I suppose the marriage will now follow out of hand. Give my compliments to Miss Finch.

What time in March may we expect your return in? I begin to be very tired of answering people's questions on that subject, and independent of that, I shall be very glad to see you at home again, and then if we can get Martha and shirk ... who will be so happy as we?

I think of going to Ibthorp in about a fortnight. My eyes are pretty well, I thank you, if you please.

Wednesday, 23d.—I wish my dear Fanny many returns of this day, and that she may on every return enjoy as much pleasure as she is now receiving from her doll's-beds.

I have just heard from Charles, who is by this time at Deal.

He is to be second lieutenant, which pleases him very well. The "Endymion" is come into the Downs, which pleases him likewise. He expects to be ordered to Sheerness shortly, as the "Tamar" has never been refitted.

My father and mother made the same match for you last night, and are very much pleased with it. *He* is a beauty of my mother's.

Yours affectionately,
JANE.

Miss AUSTEN,
Godmersham Park, Faversham, Kent.

XIV.

---

13 Queen's Square, Friday (May 17).

My dearest Cassandra,—Our journey yesterday went off exceedingly well; nothing occurred to alarm or delay us. We found the roads in excellent order, had very good horses all the way, and reached Devizes with ease by four o'clock. I suppose John has told you in what manner we were divided when we left Andover, and no alteration was afterwards made. At Devizes we had comfortable rooms and a good dinner, to which we sat down about five; amongst other things we had asparagus and a lobster, which made me wish for you, and some cheesecakes, on which the children made so delightful a supper as to endear the town of Devizes to them for a long time.

Well, here we are at Bath; we got here about one o'clock, and have been arrived just long enough to go over the house, fix on our rooms, and be very well pleased with the whole of it. Poor Elizabeth has had a dismal ride of it from Devizes, for it has rained almost all the way, and our first view of Bath has been just as gloomy as it was last November twelvemonth.

I have got so many things to say, so many things equally important, that I know not on which to decide at present, and shall therefore go and eat with the children.

We stopped in Paragon as we came along, but as it was too wet and dirty for us to get out, we could only see Frank, who told us that his master was very indifferent, but had had a better night last night than usual. In Paragon we met Mrs. Foley and Mrs. Dowdeswell with her yellow shawl airing out, and at the bottom of Kingsdown Hill we met a gentleman in a buggy, who, on minute examination, turned out to be Dr. Hall—and Dr. Hall in such very deep mourning that either his mother, his wife, or himself must be dead. These are all of our acquaintance who have yet met our eyes.

I have some hopes of being plagued about my trunk; I had more a few hours ago, for it was too heavy to go by the coach which brought Thomas and Rebecca from Devizes; there was reason to suppose that it might be too heavy likewise for any other coach, and for a long time we could hear of no wagon to convey it. At last, however, we unluckily discovered that one was just on the point of setting out for this place, but at any rate the trunk cannot be here till to-morrow; so far we are safe, and who knows what may not happen to procure a further delay?

I put Mary's letter into the post-office at Andover with my own hand.

We are exceedingly pleased with the house; the rooms are quite as large as we expected. Mrs. Bromley is a fat woman in mourning, and a little black kitten runs about the staircase. Elizabeth has the apartment within the drawing-room; she wanted my mother to have it, but as there was no bed in the inner one, and the stairs are so much easier of ascent, or my mother so much stronger than in Paragon as not to regard the double flight, it is settled for us to be above, where we have two very nice-sized rooms, with dirty quilts and everything comfortable. I have the outward and larger apartment, as I ought to have; which is quite as large as our bedroom at home, and my mother's is not materially less. The beds are both as large as any at Steventon, and I have a very nice chest of drawers and a closet full of shelves,—so full indeed that there is nothing else in it, and it should therefore be called a cupboard rather than a closet, I suppose.

Tell Mary that there were some carpenters at work in the inn at Devizes this morning, but as I could not be sure of their being Mrs. W. Fowle's relations, I did not make myself known to them.

I hope it will be a tolerable afternoon. When first we came, all the umbrellas were up, but now the pavements are getting very white again.

My mother does not seem at all the worse for her journey, nor are any of us, I hope, though Edward seemed rather fagged last night, and not very brisk this morning; but I trust the bustle of sending for tea, coffee, and sugar, etc., and going out to taste a cheese himself, will do him good.

There was a very long list of arrivals here in the newspaper yesterday, so that we need not immediately dread absolute solitude; and there is a public breakfast in Sydney Gardens every morning, so that we shall not be wholly starved.

Elizabeth has just had a very good account of the three little boys. I hope you are very busy and very comfortable. I find no difficulty in closing my eyes. I like our situation very much; it is far more cheerful than Paragon, and the prospect from the drawing-room window, at which I now write, is rather picturesque, as it commands a prospective view of the left side of Brock Street, broken by three Lombardy poplars in the garden of the last house in Queen's Parade.

I am rather impatient to know the fate of my best gown, but I suppose it will be some days before Frances can get through the trunk. In the mean time I am, with many thanks for your trouble in making it, as well as marking my silk stockings,

Yours very affectionately,
JANE.

A great deal of love from everybody.
Miss AUSTEN, Steventon, Overton, Hants.

XV.

13 QUEEN SQUARE, Sunday (June 2).

MY DEAR CASSANDRA,—I am obliged to you for two letters, one from yourself and the other from Mary, for of the latter I knew nothing till on the receipt of yours yesterday, when the pigeon-basket was examined, and I received my due. As I have written to her since the time which ought to have brought me hers, I suppose she will consider herself, as I choose to consider her, still in my debt.

I will lay out all the little judgment I have in endeavoring to get such stockings for Anna as she will approve; but I do not know that I shall execute Martha's commission at all, for I am not fond of ordering shoes; and, at any rate, they shall all have flat heels.

What must I tell you of Edward? Truth or falsehood? I will try the former, and you may choose for yourself another time. He was better yesterday than he had been for two or three days before,—about as well as while he was at Steventon. He drinks at the Hetling Pump, is to bathe to-morrow, and try electricity on Tuesday. He proposed the latter himself to Dr. Fellowes, who made no objection to it, but I fancy we are all unanimous in expecting no advantage from it. At present I have no great notion of our staying here beyond the month.

I heard from Charles last week; they were to sail on Wednesday.

My mother seems remarkably well. My uncle overwalked himself at first, and can now only travel in a chair, but is otherwise very well.

My cloak is come home. I like it very much, and can now exclaim with delight, like J. Bond at hay-harvest, "This is what I have been looking for these three years." I saw some gauzes in a shop in Bath Street yesterday at only 4*d.* a yard, but they were not so good or so pretty as mine. Flowers are very much worn, and fruit is still more the thing. Elizabeth has a bunch of strawberries, and I have seen grapes, cherries, plums, and apricots. There are likewise almonds and raisins, French plums, and tamarinds at the grocers', but I have never seen any of them in hats. A plum or greengage would cost three shillings; cherries and grapes about five, I believe, but this is at some of the dearest shops. My aunt has told me of a very cheap one, near Walcot Church, to which I shall go in quest of something for you. I have never seen an old woman at the pump-room.

Elizabeth has given me a hat, and it is not only a pretty hat, but a pretty style of hat too. It is something like Eliza's, only, instead of being all straw, half of it is narrow purple ribbon. I flatter myself, however, that you can understand very little of it from this description. Heaven forbid that I should ever offer such encouragement to explanations as to give a clear one on any occasion myself! But I must write no more of this....

I spent Friday evening with the Mapletons, and was obliged to submit to being pleased in spite of my inclination. We took a very charming walk from six to eight up Beacon Hill, and across some fields, to the village of Charlecombe, which is sweetly situated in a little green valley, as a village with such a name ought to be. Marianne is sensible and intelligent; and even Jane, considering how fair she is, is not unpleasant. We had a Miss North and a Mr. Gould of our party; the latter walked home with me after tea. He is a very young man, just entered Oxford, wears spectacles, and has heard that "Evelina" was written by Dr. Johnson.

I am afraid I cannot undertake to carry Martha's shoes home, for, though we had plenty of room in our trunks when we came, we shall have many more things to take back, and I must allow besides for my packing.

There is to be a grand gala on Tuesday evening in Sydney Gardens, a concert, with illuminations and fireworks. To the latter Elizabeth and I look forward with pleasure, and even the concert will have more than its usual charm for me, as the gardens are large enough for me to get pretty well beyond the reach of its sound. In the morning Lady Willoughby is to present the colors to some corps, or Yeomanry, or other, in the Crescent, and that such festivities may have a proper commencement, we think of going to....

I am quite pleased with Martha and Mrs. Lefroy for wanting the pattern of our caps, but I am not so well pleased with your giving it to them. Some wish, some prevailing wish, is necessary to the animation of everybody's mind, and in gratifying this you leave them to form some other which will not probably be half so innocent. I shall not forget to write to Frank. Duty and love, etc.

Yours affectionately,
JANE.

My uncle is quite surprised at my hearing from you so often; but as long as we can keep the frequency of our correspondence from Martha's uncle, we will not fear our own.

Miss AUSTEN, Steventon.

XVI.

---

13 QUEEN SQUARE, Tuesday (June 11).

MY DEAR CASSANDRA,—Your letter yesterday made me very happy. I am heartily glad that you have escaped any share in the impurities of Deane, and not sorry, as it turns out, that our stay here has been lengthened. I feel tolerably secure of our getting away next week, though it is certainly possible that we may remain till Thursday the 27th. I wonder what we shall do with all our intended visits this summer! I should like to make a compromise with Adlestrop, Harden, and Bookham, that Martha's spending the summer at Steventon should be considered as our respective visits to them all.

Edward has been pretty well for this last week, and as the waters have never disagreed with him in any respect, we are inclined to hope that he will derive advantage from them in the end. Everybody encourages us in this expectation, for they all say that the effect of the waters cannot be negative, and many are the instances in which their benefit is felt afterwards more than on the spot. He is more comfortable here than I thought he would be, and so is Elizabeth, though they will both, I believe, be very glad to get away—the latter especially, which one can't wonder at somehow. So much for Mrs. Piozzi. I had some thoughts of writing the whole of my letter in her style, but I believe I shall not.

Though you have given me unlimited powers concerning your sprig, I cannot determine what to do about it, and shall therefore in this and in every other future letter continue to ask your further directions. We have been to the cheap shop, and very cheap we found it, but there are only flowers made there, no fruit;

and as I could get four or five very pretty sprigs of the former for the same money which would procure only one Orleans plum— in short, could get more for three or four shillings than I could have means of bringing home—I cannot decide on the fruit till I hear from you again. Besides, I cannot help thinking that it is more natural to have flowers grow out of the head than fruit. What do you think on that subject?

I would not let Martha read "First Impressions"[4] again upon any account, and am very glad that I did not leave it in your power. She is very cunning, but I saw through her design; she means to publish it from memory, and one more perusal must enable her to do it. As for "Fitzalbini," when I get home she shall have it, as soon as ever she will own that Mr. Elliott is handsomer than Mr. Lance, that fair men are preferable to black; for I mean to take every opportunity of rooting out her prejudices.

Benjamin Portal is here. How charming that is! I do not exactly know why, but the phrase followed so naturally that I could not help putting it down. My mother saw him the other day, but without making herself known to him.

I am very glad you liked my lace, and so are you, and so is Martha, and we are all glad together. I have got your cloak home, which is quite delightful,—as delightful at least as half the circumstances which are called so.

I do not know what is the matter with me to-day, but I cannot write quietly; I am always wandering away into some exclamation or other. Fortunately I have nothing very particular to say.

We walked to Weston one evening last week, and liked it very much. Liked what very much? Weston? No, walking to Weston. I have not expressed myself properly, but I hope you will understand me.

We have not been to any public place lately, nor performed anything out of the common daily routine of No. 13 Queen Square, Bath. But to-day we were to have dashed away at a very extraordinary rate, by dining out, had it not so happened that we did not go.

Edward renewed his acquaintance lately with Mr. Evelyn, who lives in the Queen's Parade, and was invited to a family dinner, which I believe at first Elizabeth was rather sorry at his accepting; but yesterday Mrs. Evelyn called on us, and her manners were so pleasing that we liked the idea of going very much. The Biggs would call her a nice woman. But Mr. Evelyn, who was indisposed yesterday, is worse to-day, and we are put off.

It is rather impertinent to suggest any household care to a housekeeper, but I just venture to say that the coffee-mill will be wanted every day while Edward is at Steventon, as he always drinks coffee for breakfast.

Fanny desires her love to you, her love to grandpapa, her love to Anna, and her love to Hannah; the latter is particularly to be remembered. Edward desires his love to you, to grandpapa, to Anna, to little Edward, to Aunt James and Uncle James, and he hopes all your turkeys and ducks and chicken and guinea fowls are very well; and he wishes you very much to send him a printed letter, and so does Fanny—and they both rather think they shall answer it....

Dr. Gardiner was married yesterday to Mrs. Percy and her three daughters.

Now I will give you the history of Mary's veil, in the purchase of which I have so considerably involved you that it is my duty to economize for you in the flowers. I had no difficulty in getting a muslin veil for half a guinea, and not much more in discovering afterwards that the muslin was thick, dirty, and ragged, and therefore would by no means do for a united gift. I changed it consequently as soon as I could, and, considering what a state my imprudence had reduced me to, I thought myself lucky in getting a black lace one for sixteen shillings. I hope the half of that sum will not greatly exceed what you had intended to offer upon the altar of sister-in-law affection.

Yours affectionately,
JANE.

They do not seem to trouble you much from Manydown. I have long wanted to quarrel with them, and I believe I shall take this opportunity. There is no denying that they are very capricious—for they like to enjoy their elder sister's company when they can. Miss AUSTEN, Steventon, Overton, Hants.

FOOTNOTES:
[4] The title first chosen for "Pride and Prejudice."

XVII.

_____

STEVENTON, Thursday (November 20, 1800).

MY DEAR CASSANDRA,—Your letter took me quite by surprise this morning; you are very welcome, however, and I am very much obliged to you. I believe I drank too much wine last night at Hurstbourne; I know not how else to account for the shaking of my hand to-day. You will kindly make allowance therefore for any indistinctness of writing, by attributing it to this venial error.

Naughty Charles did not come on Tuesday, but good Charles came yesterday morning. About two o'clock he walked in on a Gosport hack. His feeling equal to such a fatigue is a good sign, and his feeling no fatigue in it a still better. He walked down to Deane to dinner; he danced the whole evening, and to-day is no more tired than a gentleman ought to be.

Your desiring to hear from me on Sunday will, perhaps, bring you a more particular account of the ball than you may care for, because one is prone to think much more of such things the morning after they happen, than when time has entirely driven them out of one's recollection.

It was a pleasant evening; Charles found it remarkably so, but I cannot tell why, unless the absence of Miss Terry, towards whom his conscience reproaches him with being now perfectly indifferent, was a relief to him. There were only twelve dances, of which I danced nine, and was merely prevented from dancing the rest by the want of a partner. We began at ten, supped at one, and were at Deane before five. There were but fifty people in the room; very few families indeed from our side of the county, and not many more from the other. My partners were the two

St. Johns, Hooper, Holder, and a very prodigious Mr. Mathew, with whom I called the last, and whom I liked the best of my little stock.

There were very few beauties, and such as there were were not very handsome. Miss Iremonger did not look well, and Mrs. Blount was the only one much admired. She appeared exactly as she did in September, with the same broad face, diamond bandeau, white shoes, pink husband, and fat neck. The two Miss Coxes were there; I traced in one the remains of the vulgar, broad-featured girl who danced at Enham eight years ago; the other is refined into a nice, composed-looking girl, like Catherine Bigg. I looked at Sir Thomas Champneys, and thought of poor Rosalie; I looked at his daughter, and thought her a queer animal with a white neck. Mrs. Warren I was constrained to think a very fine young woman, which I much regret. She danced away with great activity. Her husband is ugly enough, uglier even than his cousin John; but he does not look so *very* old. The Miss Maitlands are both prettyish, very like Anne, with brown skins, large dark eyes, and a good deal of nose. The General has got the gout, and Mrs. Maitland the jaundice. Miss Debary, Susan, and Sally, all in black, but without any statues, made their appearance, and I was as civil to them as circumstances would allow me....

Mary said that I looked very well last night. I wore my aunt's gown and handkerchief, and my hair was at least tidy, which was all my ambition. I will now have done with the ball, and I will moreover go and dress for dinner....

Farewell; Charles sends you his best love, and Edward his worst. If you think the distinction improper, you may take the worst yourself. He will write to you when he gets back to his ship, and in the mean time desires that you will consider me as

Your affectionate sister,
J. A.

Friday.—I have determined to go on Thursday, but of course not before the post comes in. Charles is in very good looks indeed. I had the comfort of finding out the other evening who all the fat girls with long noses were that disturbed me at the First H. ball. They all proved to be Miss Atkinsons of En—[*illegible*].

I rejoice to say that we have just had another letter from our dear Frank. It is to you, very short, written from Larnica in Cyprus, and so lately as October 2. He came from Alexandria, and was to return there in three or four days, knew nothing of his promotion, and does not write above twenty lines, from a doubt of the letter's ever reaching you, and an idea of all letters being opened at Vienna. He wrote a few days before to you from Alexandria by the "Mercury," sent with despatches to Lord Keith. Another letter must be owing to us besides this, one if not two; because none of these are to me. Henry comes to-morrow, for one night only.

My mother has heard from Mrs. E. Leigh. Lady Saye and Seale and her daughter are going to remove to Bath. Mrs. Estwick is married again to a Mr. Sloane, a young man under age, without the knowledge of either family. He bears a good character, however.

Miss AUSTEN,

Godmersham Park, Faversham, Kent.

XVIII.

STEVENTON, Saturday (January 3, 1801).

MY DEAR CASSANDRA,—As you have by this time received my last letter, it is fit that I should begin another; and I begin with the hope, which is at present uppermost in my mind, that you often wore a white gown in the morning at the time of all the gay parties being with you.

Our visit at Ash Park, last Wednesday, went off in a *come-cá* way. We met Mr. Lefroy and Tom Chute, played at cards, and came home again. James and Mary dined here on the following day, and at night Henry set off in the mail for London. He was as agreeable as ever during his visit, and has not lost anything in Miss Lloyd's estimation.

Yesterday we were quite alone—only our four selves; but to-day the scene is agreeably varied by Mary's driving Martha to Basingstoke, and Martha's afterwards dining at Deane.

My mother looks forward with as much certainty as you can do to our keeping two maids; my father is the only one not in the secret. We plan having a steady cook and a young giddy housemaid, with a sedate, middle-aged man, who is to undertake the double office of husband to the former and sweetheart to the latter. No children of course to be allowed on either side.

You feel more for John Bond than John Bond deserves. I am sorry to lower his character, but he is not ashamed to own himself that he has no doubt at all of getting a good place, and that he had even an offer many years ago from a Farmer Paine of taking him into his service whenever he might quit my father's.

There are three parts of Bath which we have thought of as

likely to have houses in them,—Westgate Buildings, Charles Street, and some of the short streets leading from Laura Place or Pulteney Street.

Westgate Buildings, though quite in the lower part of the town, are not badly situated themselves. The street is broad, and has rather a good appearance. Charles Street, however, I think is preferable. The buildings are new, and its nearness to Kingsmead Fields would be a pleasant circumstance. Perhaps you may remember, or perhaps you may forget, that Charles Street leads from the Queen Square Chapel to the two Green Park Streets.

The houses in the streets near Laura Place I should expect to be above our price. Gay Street would be too high, except only the lower house on the left-hand side as you ascend. Towards that my mother has no disinclination; it used to be lower rented than any other house in the row, from some inferiority in the apartments. But above all others her wishes are at present fixed on the corner house in Chapel Row, which opens into Prince's Street. Her knowledge of it, however, is confined only to the outside, and therefore she is equally uncertain of its being really desirable as of its being to be had. In the mean time she assures you that she will do everything in her power to avoid Trim Street, although you have not expressed the fearful presentiment of it which was rather expected.

We know that Mrs. Perrot will want to get us into Oxford Buildings, but we all unite in particular dislike of that part of the town, and therefore hope to escape. Upon all these different situations you and Edward may confer together, and your opinion of each will be expected with eagerness.

As to our pictures, the battle-piece, Mr. Nibbs, Sir William East, and all the old heterogeneous, miscellany, manuscript, Scriptural pieces dispersed over the house, are to be given to James. Your own drawings will not cease to be your own, and the two paintings on tin will be at your disposal. My mother says that the French agricultural prints in the best bedroom were given by Edward to his two sisters. Do you or he know anything about it?

She has written to my aunt, and we are all impatient for the answer. I do not know how to give up the idea of our both going to Paragon in May. Your going I consider as indispensably necessary, and I shall not like being left behind; there is no place here or hereabouts that I shall want to be staying at, and though, to be sure, the keep of two will be more than of one, I will endeavor to make the difference less by disordering my stomach with Bath buns; and as to the trouble of accommodating us, whether there are one or two, it is much the same.

According to the first plan, my mother and our two selves are to travel down together, and my father follow us afterwards in about a fortnight or three weeks. We have promised to spend a couple of days at Ibthorp in our way. We must all meet at Bath, you know, before we set out for the sea, and, everything considered, I think the first plan as good as any.

My father and mother, wisely aware of the difficulty of finding in all Bath such a bed as their own, have resolved on taking it with them; all the beds, indeed, that we shall want are to be removed,—namely, besides theirs, our own two, the best for a spare one, and two for servants; and these necessary articles will probably be the only material ones that it would answer to send down. I do not think it will be worth while to remove any of our chests of drawers; we shall be able to get some of a much more commodious sort, made of deal, and painted to look very neat; and I flatter myself that for little comforts of all kinds our apartment will be one of the most complete things of the sort all over Bath, Bristol included.

We have thought at times of removing the sideboard, or a Pembroke table, or some other piece of furniture, but, upon the whole, it has ended in thinking that the trouble and risk of the removal would be more than the advantage of having them at a place where everything may be purchased. Pray send your opinion.

Martha has as good as promised to come to us again in March. Her spirits are better than they were....

My mother bargains for having no trouble at all in furnishing our house in Bath, and I have engaged for your willingly undertaking to do it all. I get more and more reconciled to the idea of our removal. We have lived long enough in this neighborhood: the Basingstoke balls are certainly on the decline, there is something interesting in the bustle of going away, and the prospect of spending future summers by the sea or in Wales is very delightful. For a time we shall now possess many of the advantages which I have often thought of with envy in the wives of sailors or soldiers. It must not be generally known, however, that I am not sacrificing a great deal in quitting the country, or I can expect to inspire no tenderness, no interest, in those we leave behind....

Yours affectionately,
J. A.

Miss AUSTEN,
Godmersham Park, Faversham, Kent.

XIX.

STEVENTON, Thursday (January 8).

MY DEAR CASSANDRA,—The "perhaps" which concluded my last letter being only a "perhaps," will not occasion your being overpowered with surprise, I dare say, if you should receive this before Tuesday, which, unless circumstances are very perverse, will be the case. I received yours with much general philanthropy, and still more peculiar good-will, two days ago; and I suppose I need not tell you that it was very long, being written on a foolscap sheet, and very entertaining, being written by you.

Mr. Payne has been dead long enough for Henry to be out of mourning for him before his last visit, though we knew nothing of it till about that time. Why he died, or of what complaint, or to what noblemen he bequeathed his four daughters in marriage, we have not heard.

I am glad that the Wildmans are going to give a ball, and hope you will not fail to benefit both yourself and me by laying out a few kisses in the purchase of a frank. I believe you are right in proposing to delay the cambric muslin, and I submit with a kind of voluntary reluctance.

Mr. Peter Debary has declined Deane curacy; he wishes to be settled near London. A foolish reason! as if Deane were not near London in comparison of Exeter or York. Take the whole world through, and he will find many more places at a greater distance from London than Deane than he will at a less. What does he think of Glencoe or Lake Katherine?

I feel rather indignant that any possible objection should be raised against so valuable a piece of preferment, so delightful a situation!—that Deane should not be universally allowed to be as near the metropolis as any other country villages. As this is the case, however, as Mr. Peter Debary has shown himself a Peter in the blackest sense of the word, we are obliged to look elsewhere for an heir; and my father has thought it a necessary compliment to James Digweed to offer the curacy to him, though without considering it as either a desirable or an eligible situation for him. Unless he is in love with Miss Lyford, I think he had better not be settled exactly in this neighborhood; and unless he is very much in love with her indeed, he is not likely to think a salary of 50*l*. equal in value or efficiency to one of 75*l*.

Were you indeed to be considered as one of the fixtures of the house!—but you were never actually erected in it either by Mr. Egerton Brydges or Mrs. Lloyd....

You are very kind in planning presents for me to make, and my mother has shown me exactly the same attention; but as I do not choose to have generosity dictated to me, I shall not resolve on giving my cabinet to Anna till the first thought of it has been my own.

Sidmouth is now talked of as our summer abode. Get all the information, therefore, about it that you can from Mrs. C. Cage.

My father's old ministers are already deserting him to pay their court to his son. The brown mare, which, as well as the black, was to devolve on James at our removal, has not had patience to wait for that, and has settled herself even now at Deane. The death of Hugh Capet, which, like that of Mr. Skipsey, though undesired, was not wholly unexpected, being purposely effected, has made the immediate possession of the mare very convenient, and everything else I suppose will be seized by degrees in the same manner. Martha and I work at the books every day.

Yours affectionately,
J. A.

Miss AUSTEN,
Godmersham Park, Faversham, Kent.

XX.

_____

STEVENTON, Wednesday (January 14).

POOR Miss Austen! It appears to me that I have rather oppressed you of late by the frequency of my letters. You had hoped not to hear from me again before Tuesday, but Sunday showed you with what a merciless sister you had to deal. I cannot recall the past, but you shall not hear from me quite so often in future.

Your letter to Mary was duly received before she left Deane with Martha yesterday morning, and it gives us great pleasure to know that the Chilham ball was so agreeable, and that you danced four dances with Mr. Kemble. Desirable, however, as the latter circumstance was, I cannot help wondering at its taking place. Why did you dance four dances with so stupid a man? Why not rather dance two of them with some elegant brother officer who was struck with your appearance as soon as you entered the room?

Martha left you her best love. She will write to you herself in a short time; but trusting to my memory rather than her own, she has nevertheless desired me to ask you to purchase for her two bottles of Steele's lavender water when you are in town, provided you should go to the shop on your own account, otherwise you may be sure that she would not have you recollect the request.

James dined with us yesterday, wrote to Edward in the evening, filled three sides of paper, every line inclining too much towards the northeast, and the very first line of all scratched out, and this morning he joins his lady in the fields of Elysium and Ibthorp.

Last Friday was a very busy day with us. We were visited by Miss Lyford and Mr. Bayle. The latter began his operations in the house, but had only time to finish the four sitting-rooms; the rest is deferred till the spring is more advanced and the days longer. He took his paper of appraisement away with him, and therefore we only know the estimate he has made of one or two articles of furniture which my father particularly inquired into. I understand, however, that he was of opinion that the whole would amount to more than two hundred pounds, and it is not imagined that this will comprehend the brewhouse and many other, etc., etc.

Miss Lyford was very pleasant, and gave my mother such an account of the houses in Westgate Buildings, where Mrs. Lyford lodged four years ago, as made her think of a situation there with great pleasure, but your opposition will be without difficulty decisive, and my father, in particular, who was very well inclined towards the Row before, has now ceased to think of it entirely. At present the environs of Laura Place seem to be his choice. His views on the subject are much advanced since I came home; he grows quite ambitious, and actually requires now a comfortable and a creditable-looking house.

On Saturday Miss Lyford went to her long home,—that is to say, it was a long way off,—and soon afterwards a party of fine ladies issuing from a well-known commodious green vehicle, their heads full of Bantam cocks and Galinies, entered the house,—Mrs. Heathcote, Mrs. Harwood, Mrs. James Austen, Miss Bigg, Miss Jane Blachford.

Hardly a day passes in which we do not have some visitor or other: yesterday came Mrs. Bramstone, who is very sorry that she is to lose us, and afterwards Mr. Holder, who was shut up for an hour with my father and James in a most awful manner. John Bond *est à lui....*

XXI.

STEVENTON, Wednesday (January 21).

EXPECT a most agreeable letter, for not being overburdened with subject (having nothing at all to say), I shall have no check to my genius from beginning to end.

Well, and so Prank's letter has made you very happy, but you are afraid he would not have patience to stay for the "Haarlem," which you wish him to have done as being safer than the merchantman. Poor fellow! to wait from the middle of November to the end of December, and perhaps even longer, it must be sad work; especially in a place where the ink is so abominably pale. What a surprise to him it must have been on October 20, to be visited, collared, and thrust out of the "Petterel" by Captain Inglis. He kindly passes over the poignancy of his feelings in quitting his ship, his officers, and his men.

What a pity it is that he should not be in England at the time of this promotion, because he certainly would have had an appointment, so everybody says, and therefore it must be right for me to say it too. Had he been really here, the certainty of the appointment, I dare say, would not have been half so great, but as it could not be brought to the proof, his absence will be always a lucky source of regret.

Eliza talks of having read in a newspaper that all the first lieutenants of the frigates whose captains were to be sent into line-of-battle ships were to be promoted to the rank of commanders. If it be true, Mr. Valentine may afford himself a fine Valentine's knot, and Charles may perhaps become first of the "Endymion," though I suppose Captain Durham is too likely to bring a villain with him under that denomination....

The neighborhood have quite recovered the death of Mrs. Rider,—so much so, that I think they are rather rejoiced at it now; her things were so very dear! and Mrs. Rogers is to be all that is desirable. Not even death itself can fix the friendship of the world....

The Wylmots being robbed must be an amusing thing to their acquaintance, and I hope it is as much their pleasure as it seems their avocation to be subjects of general entertainment.

I have a great mind not to acknowledge the receipt of your letter, which I have just had the pleasure of reading, because I am so ashamed to compare the sprawling lines of this with it. But if I say all that I have to say, I hope I have no reason to hang myself....

Why did not J. D. make his proposals to you? I suppose he went to see the cathedral, that he might know how he should like to be married in it....

Miss AUSTEN,
Godmersham Park, Faversham, Kent.

XXII.

SOUTHAMPTON, Wednesday (January 7, 1807).

MY DEAR CASSANDRA,—You were mistaken in supposing I should expect your letter on Sunday; I had no idea of hearing from you before Tuesday, and my pleasure yesterday was therefore unhurt by any previous disappointment. I thank you for writing so much; you must really have sent me the value of two letters in one. We are extremely glad to hear that Elizabeth is so much better, and hope you will be sensible of still further amendment in her when you return from Canterbury.

Of your visit there I must now speak "incessantly;" it surprises, but pleases me more, and I consider it as a very just and honorable distinction of you, and not less to the credit of Mrs. Knight. I have no doubt of your spending your time with her most pleasantly in quiet and rational conversation, and am so far from thinking her expectations of you will be deceived, that my only fear is of your being so agreeable, so much to her taste, as to make her wish to keep you with her forever. If that should be the case, we must remove to Canterbury, which I should not like so well as Southampton.

When you receive this, our guests will be all gone or going; and I shall be left to the comfortable disposal of my time, to ease of mind from the torments of rice puddings and apple dumplings, and probably to regret that I did not take more pains to please them all.

Mrs. J. Austen has asked me to return with her to Steventon; I need not give my answer; and she has invited my mother to spend there the time of Mrs. F. A.'s confinement, which she seems half inclined to do.

A few days ago I had a letter from Miss Irvine, and as I was in her debt, you will guess it to be a remonstrance, not a very severe one, however; the first page is in her usual retrospective, jealous, inconsistent style, but the remainder is chatty and harmless. She supposes my silence may have proceeded from resentment of her not having written to inquire particularly after my hooping-cough, etc. She is a funny one.

I have answered her letter, and have endeavored to give something like the truth with as little incivility as I could, by placing my silence to the want of subject in the very quiet way in which we live. Phebe has repented, and stays. I have also written to Charles, and I answered Miss Buller's letter by return of post, as I intended to tell you in my last.

Two or three things I recollected when it was too late, that I might have told you; one is that the Welbys have lost their eldest son by a putrid fever at Eton, and another that Tom Chute is going to settle in Norfolk.

You have scarcely ever mentioned Lizzy since your being at Godmersham. I hope it is not because she is altered for the worse.

I cannot yet satisfy Fanny as to Mrs. Foote's baby's name, and I must not encourage her to expect a good one, as Captain Foote is a professed adversary to all but the plainest; he likes only Mary, Elizabeth, Anne, etc. Our best chance is of "Caroline," which in compliment to a sister seems the only exception.

He dined with us on Friday, and I fear will not soon venture again, for the strength of our dinner was a boiled leg of mutton, underdone even for James; and Captain Foote has a particular dislike to underdone mutton; but he was so good-humored and pleasant that I did not much mind his being starved. He gives us all the most cordial invitation to his house in the country, saying just what the Williams ought to say to make us welcome. Of them we have seen nothing since you left us, and we hear that they are just gone to Bath again, to be out of the way of further alterations at Brooklands.

Mrs. F. A. has had a very agreeable letter from Mrs. Dickson, who was delighted with the purse, and desires her not to provide herself with a christening dress, which is exactly what her young correspondent wanted; and she means to defer making any of the caps as long as she can, in hope of having Mrs. D.'s present in time to be serviceable as a pattern. She desires me to tell you that the gowns were cut out before your letter arrived, but that they are long enough for Caroline. The *Beds*, as I believe they are called, have fallen to Frank's share to continue, and of course are cut out to admiration.

"Alphonsine" did not do. We were disgusted in twenty pages, as, independent of a bad translation, it has indelicacies which disgrace a pen hitherto so pure; and we changed it for the "Female Quixote," which now makes our evening amusement; to me a very high one, as I find the work quite equal to what I remembered it. Mrs. F. A., to whom it is new, enjoys it as one could wish; the other Mary, I believe, has little pleasure from that or any other book.

My mother does not seem at all more disappointed than ourselves at the termination of the family treaty; she thinks less of that just now than of the comfortable state of her own finances, which she finds on closing her year's accounts beyond her expectation, as she begins the new year with a balance of 30*l*. in her favor; and when she has written her answer to my aunt, which you know always hangs a little upon her mind, she will be above the world entirely. You will have a great deal of unreserved discourse with Mrs. K., I dare say, upon this subject, as well as upon many other of our family matters. Abuse everybody but me.

Thursday.—We expected James yesterday, but he did not come; if he comes at all now, his visit will be a very short one, as he must return to-morrow, that Ajax and the chair may be sent to Winchester on Saturday. Caroline's new pelisse depended upon her mother's being able or not to come so far in the chair; how the guinea that will be saved by the same means of return is to be spent I know not. Mrs. J. A. does not talk much of poverty now, though she has no hope of my brother's being able to buy another horse next summer.

Their scheme against Warwickshire continues, but I doubt the family's being at Stoneleigh so early as James says he must go, which is May.

My mother is afraid I have not been explicit enough on the subject of her wealth; she began 1806 with 68*l.* she begins 1807 with 99*l.*, and this after 32*l.* purchase of stock. Frank too has been settling his accounts and making calculations, and each party feels quite equal to our present expenses; but much increase of house-rent would not do for either. Frank limits himself, I believe, to four hundred a year.

You will be surprised to hear that Jenny is not yet come back; we have heard nothing of her since her reaching Itchingswell, and can only suppose that she must be detained by illness in somebody or other, and that she has been each day expecting to be able to come on the morrow. I am glad I did not know beforehand that she was to be absent during the whole or almost the whole of our friends being with us, for though the inconvenience has not been nothing, I should have feared still more. Our dinners have certainly suffered not a little by having only Molly's head and Molly's hands to conduct them; she fries better than she did, but not like Jenny.

We did *not* take our walk on Friday, it was too dirty, nor have we yet done it; we may perhaps do something like it to-day, as after seeing Frank skate, which he hopes to do in the meadows by the beech, we are to treat ourselves with a passage over the ferry. It is one of the pleasantest frosts I ever knew, so very quiet. I hope it will last some time longer for Frank's sake, who is quite anxious to get some skating; he tried yesterday, but it would not do.

Our acquaintance increase too fast. He was recognized lately by Admiral Bertie, and a few days since arrived the Admiral and his daughter Catherine to wait upon us. There was nothing to like or dislike in either. To the Berties are to be added the Lances, with whose cards we have been endowed, and whose visit Frank and I returned yesterday. They live about a mile and three-quarters from S. to the right of the new road to Portsmouth, and I believe their house is one of those which are to be seen almost anywhere among the woods on the other side of the Itchen. It is a handsome building, stands high, and in a very beautiful situation.

We found only Mrs. Lance at home, and whether she boasts any offspring besides a grand pianoforte did not appear. She was civil and chatty enough, and offered to introduce us to some acquaintance in Southampton, which we gratefully declined.

I suppose they must be acting by the orders of Mr. Lance of Netherton in this civility, as there seems no other reason for their coming near us. They will not come often, I dare say. They live in a handsome style and are rich, and she seemed to like to be rich, and we gave her to understand that we were far from being so; she will soon feel therefore that we are not worth her acquaintance.

You must have heard from Martha by this time. We have had no accounts of Kintbury since her letter to me.

Mrs. F. A. has had one fainting fit lately; it came on as usual after eating a hearty dinner, but did not last long.

I can recollect nothing more to say. When my letter is gone, I suppose I shall.

Yours affectionately,

J. A.

I have just asked Caroline if I should send her love to her godmamma, to which she answered "Yes."

Miss AUSTEN,
Godmersham Park, Faversham, Kent.

XXIII.

SOUTHAMPTON, February 8.

... OUR garden is putting in order by a man who bears a remarkably good character, has a very fine complexion, and asks something less than the first. The shrubs which border the gravel walk, he says, are only sweetbrier and roses, and the latter of an indifferent sort; we mean to get a few of a better kind, therefore, and at my own particular desire he procures us some syringas. I could not do without a syringa, for the sake of Cowper's line. We talk also of a laburnum. The border under the terrace wall is clearing away to receive currants and gooseberry bushes, and a spot is found very proper for raspberries.

The alterations and improvements within doors, too, advance very properly, and the offices will be made very convenient indeed. Our dressing-table is constructing on the spot, out of a large kitchen table belonging to the house, for doing which we have the permission of Mr. Husket, Lord Lansdown's painter,— domestic painter, I should call him, for he lives in the castle. Domestic chaplains have given way to this more necessary office, and I suppose whenever the walls want no touching up he is employed about my lady's face.

The morning was so wet that I was afraid we should not be able to see our little visitor; but Frank, who alone could go to church, called for her after service, and she is now talking away at my side and examining the treasures of my writing-desk drawers,—very happy, I believe. Not at all shy, of course. Her name is Catherine, and her sister's Caroline. She is something like her brother, and as short for her age, but not so well-looking.

What is become of all the shyness in the world? Moral as well as natural diseases disappear in the progress of time, and new ones take their place. Shyness and the sweating sickness have given way to confidence and paralytic complaints....

Evening.—Our little visitor has just left us, and left us highly pleased with her; she is a nice, natural, open-hearted, affectionate girl, with all the ready civility which one sees in the best children in the present day; so unlike anything that I was myself at her age, that I am often all astonishment and shame. Half her time was spent at spillikins, which I consider as a very valuable part of our household furniture, and as not the least important benefaction from the family of Knight to that of Austen.

But I must tell you a story. Mary has for some time had notice from Mrs. Dickson of the intended arrival of a certain Miss Fowler in this place. Miss F. is an intimate friend of Mrs. D., and a good deal known as such to Mary. On Thursday last she called here while we were out. Mary found, on our return, her card with only her name on it, and she had left word that she would call again. The particularity of this made us talk, and, among other conjectures, Frank said in joke, "I dare say she is staying with the Pearsons." The connection of the names struck Mary, and she immediately recollected Miss Fowler's having been very intimate with persons so called, and, upon putting everything together, we have scarcely a doubt of her being actually staying with the only family in the place whom we cannot visit.

What a *contretemps!* in the language of France. What an unluckiness! in that of Madame Duval. The black gentleman has certainly employed one of his menial imps to bring about this complete, though trifling mischief. Miss F. has never called again, but we are in daily expectation of it. Miss P. has, of course, given her a proper understanding of the business. It is evident that Miss F. did not expect or wish to have the visit returned, and Frank is quite as much on his guard for his wife as we could desire for her sake or our own.

We shall rejoice in being so near Winchester when Edward belongs to it, and can never have our spare bed filled more to our satisfaction than by him. Does he leave Eltham at Easter?

We are reading "Clarentine," and are surprised to find how foolish it is. I remember liking it much less on a second reading than at the first, and it does not bear a third at all. It is full of unnatural conduct and forced difficulties, without striking merit of any kind.

Miss Harrison is going into Devonshire, to attend Mrs. Dusantoy, as usual. Miss J. is married to young Mr. G., and is to be very unhappy. He swears, drinks, is cross, jealous, selfish, and brutal. The match makes her family miserable, and has occasioned his being disinherited.

The Browns are added to our list of acquaintance. He commands the Sea Fencibles here, under Sir Thomas, and was introduced at his own desire by the latter when we saw him last week. As yet the gentlemen only have visited, as Mrs. B. is ill; but she is a nice-looking woman, and wears one of the prettiest straw bonnets in the place.

Monday.—The garret beds are made, and ours will be finished to-day. I had hoped it would be finished on Saturday, but neither Mrs. Hall nor Jenny was able to give help enough for that, and I have as yet done very little, and Mary nothing at all. This week we shall do more, and I should like to have all the five beds completed by the end of it. There will then be the window-curtains, sofa-cover, and a carpet to be altered.

I should not be surprised if we were to be visited by James again this week; he gave us reason to expect him soon, and if they go to Eversley he cannot come next week.

There, I flatter myself I have constructed you a smartish letter, considering my want of materials; but, like my dear Dr. Johnson, I believe I have dealt more in notions than facts.

I hope your cough is gone, and that you are otherwise well, and remain, with love,

Yours affectionately,
J. A.

Miss AUSTEN,
Godmersham Park, Faversham, Kent.

XXIV.

GODMERSHAM, Wednesday (June 15, 1808).

MY DEAR CASSANDRA,—Where shall I begin? Which of all my important nothings shall I tell you first? At half after seven yesterday morning Henry saw us into our own carriage, and we drove away from the Bath Hotel; which, by the by, had been found most uncomfortable quarters,—very dirty, very noisy, and very ill-provided. James began his journey by the coach at five. Our first eight miles were hot; Deptford Hill brought to my mind our hot journey into Kent fourteen years ago; but after Blackheath we suffered nothing, and as the day advanced it grew quite cool. At Dartford, which we reached within the two hours and three-quarters, we went to the Bull, the same inn at which we breakfasted in that said journey, and on the present occasion had about the same bad butter.

At half-past ten we were again off, and, travelling on without any adventure reached Sittingbourne by three. Daniel was watching for us at the door of the George, and I was acknowledged very kindly by Mr. and Mrs. Marshall, to the latter of whom I devoted my conversation, while Mary went out to buy some gloves. A few minutes, of course, did for Sittingbourne; and so off we drove, drove, drove, and by six o'clock were at Godmersham.

Our two brothers were walking before the house as we approached, as natural as life. Fanny and Lizzy met us in the Hall with a great deal of pleasant joy; we went for a few minutes into the breakfast-parlor, and then proceeded to our rooms. Mary has the Hall chamber. I am in the Yellow room—very literally—for I am writing in it at this moment. It seems odd to me to have such a great place all to myself, and to be at Godmersham without you is also odd.

You are wished for, I assure you: Fanny, who came to me as soon as she had seen her Aunt James to her room, and stayed while I dressed, was as energetic as usual in her longings for you. She is grown both in height and size since last year, but not immoderately, looks very well, and seems as to conduct and manner just what she was and what one could wish her to continue.

Elizabeth,[5] who was dressing when we arrived, came to me for a minute attended by Marianne, Charles, and Louisa, and, you will not doubt, gave me a very affectionate welcome. That I had received such from Edward also I need not mention; but I do, you see, because it is a pleasure. I never saw him look in better health, and Fanny says he is perfectly well. I cannot praise Elizabeth's looks, but they are probably affected by a cold. Her little namesake has gained in beauty in the last three years, though not all that Marianne has lost. Charles is not quite so lovely as he was. Louisa is much as I expected, and Cassandra I find handsomer than I expected, though at present disguised by such a violent breaking-out that she does not come down after dinner. She has charming eyes and a nice open countenance, and seems likely to be very lovable. Her size is magnificent.

I was agreeably surprised to find Louisa Bridges still here. She looks remarkably well (legacies are very wholesome diet), and is just what she always was. John is at Sandling. You may fancy our dinner-party therefore; Fanny, of course, belonging to it, and little Edward, for that day. He was almost too happy, his happiness at least made him too talkative.

It has struck ten; I must go to breakfast.

Since breakfast I have had a *tête-à-tête* with Edward in his room; he wanted to know James's plans and mine, and from what his own now are I think it already nearly certain that I shall return when they do, though not with them. Edward will be going about the same time to Alton, where he has business with Mr. Trimmer, and where he means his son should join him; and I shall probably be his companion to that place, and get on afterwards somehow or other.

I should have preferred a rather longer stay here certainly, but there is no prospect of any later conveyance for me, as he does not mean to accompany Edward on his return to Winchester, from a very natural unwillingness to leave Elizabeth at that time. I shall at any rate be glad not to be obliged to be an incumbrance on those who have brought me here, for, as James has no horse, I must feel in their carriage that I am taking his place. We were rather crowded yesterday, though it does not become me to say so, as I and my boa were of the party, and it is not to be supposed but that a child of three years of age was fidgety.

I need scarcely beg you to keep all this to yourself, lest it should get round by Anna's means. She is very kindly inquired after by her friends here, who all regret her not coming with her father and mother.

I left Henry, I hope, free from his tiresome complaint, in other respects well, and thinking with great pleasure of Cheltenham and Stoneleigh.

The brewery scheme is quite at an end: at a meeting of the subscribers last week it was by general, and I believe very hearty, consent dissolved.

The country is very beautiful. I saw as much as ever to admire in my yesterday's journey....

FOOTNOTES:

[5] Mrs. Edward Austen.

XXV.

———————————

CASTLE SQUARE, October 13.

MY DEAREST CASSANDRA,—I have received your letter, and with most melancholy anxiety was it expected, for the sad news[6] reached us last night, but without any particulars. It came in a short letter to Martha from her sister, begun at Steventon and finished in Winchester.

We have felt, we do feel, for you all, as you will not need to be told,—for you, for Fanny, for Henry, for Lady Bridges, and for dearest Edward, whose loss and whose sufferings seem to make those of every other person nothing. God be praised that you can say what you do of him: that he has a religious mind to bear him up, and a disposition that will gradually lead him to comfort.

My dear, dear Fanny, I am so thankful that she has you with her! You will be everything to her; you will give her all the consolation that human aid can give. May the Almighty sustain you all, and keep you, my dearest Cassandra, well; but for the present I dare say you are equal to everything.

You will know that the poor boys are at Steventon. Perhaps it is best for them, as they will have more means of exercise and amusement there than they could have with us, but I own myself disappointed by the arrangement. I should have loved to have them with me at such a time. I shall write to Edward by this post.

We shall, of course, hear from you again very soon, and as often as you can write. We will write as you desire, and I shall add Bookham. Hamstall, I suppose, you write to yourselves, as you do not mention it.

What a comfort that Mrs. Deedes is saved from present misery and alarm! But it will fall heavy upon poor Harriot; and as for Lady B., but that her fortitude does seem truly great, I should fear the effect of such a blow, and so unlooked for. I long to hear more of you all. Of Henry's anguish I think with grief and solicitude; but he will exert himself to be of use and comfort.

With what true sympathy our feelings are shared by Martha you need not be told; she is the friend and sister under every circumstance.

We need not enter into a panegyric on the departed, but it is sweet to think of her great worth, of her solid principles, of her true devotion, her excellence in every relation of life. It is also consolatory to reflect on the shortness of the sufferings which led her from this world to a better.

Farewell for the present, my dearest sister. Tell Edward that we feel for him and pray for him.

Yours affectionately,
J. AUSTEN.

I will write to Catherine.

Perhaps you can give me some directions about mourning.

Miss AUSTEN, EDWARD AUSTEN'S, Esq.,
Godmersham Park, Faversham, Kent.

FOOTNOTE:

[6] The death of Mrs. Edward Austen.

XXVI.

CASTLE SQUARE, Saturday night (October 15).

MY DEAR CASSANDRA,—Your accounts make us as comfortable as we can expect to be at such a time. Edward's loss is terrible, and must be felt as such, and these are too early days indeed to think of moderation in grief, either in him or his afflicted daughter, but soon we may hope that our dear Fanny's sense of duty to that beloved father will rouse her to exertion. For his sake, and as the most acceptable proof of love to the spirit of her departed mother, she will try to be tranquil and resigned. Does she feel you to be a comfort to her, or is she too much overpowered for anything but solitude?

Your account of Lizzy is very interesting. Poor child! One must hope the impression will be strong, and yet one's heart aches for a dejected mind of eight years old.

I suppose you see the corpse? How does it appear? We are anxious to be assured that Edward will not attend the funeral, but when it comes to the point I think he must feel it impossible.

Your parcel shall set off on Monday, and I hope the shoes will fit; Martha and I both tried them on. I shall send you such of your mourning as I think most likely to be useful, reserving for myself your stockings and half the velvet, in which selfish arrangement I know I am doing what you wish.

I am to be in bombazeen and crape, according to what we are told is universal here, and which agrees with Martha's previous observation. My mourning, however, will not impoverish me, for by having my velvet pelisse fresh lined and made up, I am sure I shall have no occasion this winter for anything new of that sort. I take my cloak for the lining, and shall send yours on the chance of its doing something of the same for you, though I believe your pelisse is in better repair than mine. One Miss Baker makes my gown and the other my bonnet, which is to be silk covered with crape.

I have written to Edward Cooper, and hope he will not send one of his letters of cruel comfort to my poor brother: and yesterday I wrote to Alethea Bigg, in reply to a letter from her. She tells us in confidence that Catherine is to be married on Tuesday se'nnight. Mr. Hill is expected at Manydown in the course of the ensuing week.

We are desired by Mrs. Harrison and Miss Austen to say everything proper for them to yourself and Edward on this sad occasion, especially that nothing but a wish of not giving additional trouble where so much is inevitable prevents their writing themselves to express their concern. They seem truly to feel concern.

I am glad you can say what you do of Mrs. Knight and of Goodnestone in general. It is a great relief to me to know that the shock did not make any of them ill. But what a task was yours to announce it! Now I hope you are not overpowered with letter-writing, as Henry and John can ease you of many of your correspondents.

Was Mr. Scudamore in the house at the time, was any application attempted, and is the seizure at all accounted for?

Sunday.—As Edward's letter to his son is not come here, we know that you must have been informed as early as Friday of the boys being at Steventon, which I am glad of.

Upon your letter to Dr. Goddard's being forwarded to them, Mary wrote to ask whether my mother wished to have her grandsons sent to her. We decided on their remaining where they were, which I hope my brother will approve of. I am sure he will do us the justice of believing that in such a decision we sacrificed inclination to what we thought best.

I shall write by the coach to-morrow to Mrs. J. A., and to

Edward, about their mourning, though this day's post will probably bring directions to them on that subject from yourselves. I shall certainly make use of the opportunity of addressing our nephew on the most serious of all concerns, as I naturally did in my letter to him before. The poor boys are, perhaps, more comfortable at Steventon than they could be here, but you will understand my feelings with respect to it.

To-morrow will be a dreadful day for you all. Mr. Whitfield's will be a severe duty.[7] Glad shall I be to hear that it is over.

That you are forever in our thoughts you will not doubt. I see your mournful party in my mind's eye under every varying circumstance of the day; and in the evening especially figure to myself its sad gloom: the efforts to talk, the frequent summons to melancholy orders and cares, and poor Edward, restless in misery, going from one room to another, and perhaps not seldom upstairs, to see all that remains of his Elizabeth. Dearest Fanny must now look upon herself as his prime source of comfort, his dearest friend; as the being who is gradually to supply to him, to the extent that is possible, what he has lost. This consideration will elevate and cheer her.

Adieu. You cannot write too often, as I said before. We are heartily rejoiced that the poor baby gives you no particular anxiety. Kiss dear Lizzy for us. Tell Fanny that I shall write in a day or two to Miss Sharpe.

My mother is not ill.

Yours most truly,
J. AUSTEN.

Tell Henry that a hamper of apples is gone to him from Kintbury, and that Mr. Fowle intended writing on Friday (supposing him in London) to beg that the charts, etc., may be consigned to the care of the Palmers. Mrs. Fowle has also written to Miss Palmer to beg she will send for them.

Miss AUSTEN, EDWARD AUSTEN'S, Esq.,
Godmersham Park, Faversham, Kent.

FOOTNOTE:

[7] Mr. Whitfield was the Rector of Godmersham at this time,
having come there in 1778.

XXVII.

CASTLE SQUARE, Monday (October 24).

MY DEAR CASSANDRA,—Edward and George came to us soon after seven on Saturday, very well, but very cold, having by choice travelled on the outside, and with no greatcoat but what Mr. Wise, the coachman, good-naturedly spared them of his, as they sat by his side. They were so much chilled when they arrived, that I was afraid they must have taken cold; but it does not seem at all the case: I never saw them looking better.

They behave extremely well in every respect, showing quite as much feeling as one wishes to see, and on every occasion speaking of their father with the liveliest affection. His letter was read over by each of them yesterday, and with many tears; George sobbed aloud, Edward's tears do not flow so easily; but as far as I can judge they are both very properly impressed by what has happened. Miss Lloyd, who is a more impartial judge than I can be, is exceedingly pleased with them.

George is almost a new acquaintance to me, and I find him in a different way as engaging as Edward.

We do not want amusement: bilbocatch, at which George is indefatigable, spillikins, paper ships, riddles, conundrums, and cards, with watching the flow and ebb of the river, and now and then a stroll out, keep us well employed; and we mean to avail ourselves of our kind papa's consideration, by not returning to Winchester till quite the evening of Wednesday.

Mrs. J. A. had not time to get them more than one suit of clothes; their others are making here, and though I do not believe Southampton is famous for tailoring, I hope it will prove itself better than Basingstoke. Edward has an old black coat, which will save his having a second new one; but I find that black pantaloons are considered by them as necessary, and of course one would not have them made uncomfortable by the want of what is usual on such occasions.

Fanny's letter was received with great pleasure yesterday, and her brother sends his thanks and will answer it soon. We all saw what she wrote, and were very much pleased with it.

To-morrow I hope to hear from you, and to-morrow we must think of poor Catherine. To-day Lady Bridges is the heroine of our thoughts, and glad shall we be when we can fancy the meeting over. There will then be nothing so very bad for Edward to undergo.

The "St. Albans," I find, sailed on the very day of my letters reaching Yarmouth, so that we must not expect an answer at present; we scarcely feel, however, to be in suspense, or only enough to keep our plans to ourselves. We have been obliged to explain them to our young visitors, in consequence of Fanny's letter, but we have not yet mentioned them to Steventon. We are all quite familiarized to the idea ourselves; my mother only wants Mrs. Seward to go out at midsummer.

What sort of a kitchen garden is there? Mrs. J. A. expresses her fear of our settling in Kent, and, till this proposal was made, we began to look forward to it here; my mother was actually talking of a house at Wye. It will be best, however, as it is.

Anne has just given her mistress warning; she is going to be married; I wish she would stay her year.

On the subject of matrimony, I must notice a wedding in the Salisbury paper, which has amused me very much, Dr. Phillot to Lady Frances St. Lawrence. She wanted to have a husband, I suppose, once in her life, and he a Lady Frances.

I hope your sorrowing party were at church yesterday, and have no longer that to dread. Martha was kept at home by a cold, but I went with my two nephews, and I saw Edward was much affected by the sermon, which, indeed, I could have supposed purposely addressed to the afflicted, if the text had not naturally come in the course of Dr. Mant's observations on the Litany: 'All that are in danger, necessity, or tribulation,' was the subject of it. The weather did not allow us afterwards to get farther than the quay, where George was very happy as long as we could stay, flying about from one side to the other, and skipping on board a collier immediately.

In the evening we had the Psalms and Lessons, and a sermon at home, to which they were very attentive; but you will not expect to hear that they did not return to conundrums the moment it was over. Their aunt has written pleasantly of them, which was more than I hoped.

While I write now, George is most industriously making and naming paper ships, at which he afterwards shoots with horse-chestnuts, brought from Steventon on purpose; and Edward equally intent over the "Lake of Killarney," twisting himself about in one of our great chairs.

Tuesday.—Your close-written letter makes me quite ashamed of my wide lines; you have sent me a great deal of matter, most of it very welcome. As to your lengthened stay, it is no more than I expected, and what must be, but you cannot suppose I like it.

All that you say of Edward is truly comfortable; I began to fear that when the bustle of the first week was over, his spirits might for a time be more depressed; and perhaps one must still expect something of the kind. If you escape a bilious attack, I shall wonder almost as much as rejoice. I am glad you mentioned where Catherine goes to-day; it is a good plan, but sensible people may generally be trusted to form such.

The day began cheerfully, but it is not likely to continue what it should, for them or for us. We had a little water-party yesterday; I and my two nephews went from the Itchen Ferry up to Northam, where we landed, looked into the 74, and walked home, and it was so much enjoyed that I had intended to take them to Netley to-day; the tide is just right for our going immediately after moonshine, but I am afraid there will be rain; if we cannot get so far, however, we may perhaps go round from the ferry to the quay.

I had not proposed doing more than cross the Itchen yesterday, but it proved so pleasant, and so much to the satisfaction of all, that when we reached the middle of the stream we agreed to be rowed up the river; both the boys rowed great part of the way, and their questions and remarks, as well as their enjoyment, were very amusing; George's inquiries were endless, and his eagerness in everything reminds me often of his uncle Henry.

Our evening was equally agreeable in its way: I introduced speculation, and it was so much approved that we hardly knew how to leave off.

Your idea of an early dinner to-morrow is exactly what we propose, for, after writing the first part of this letter, it came into my head that at this time of year we have not summer evenings. We shall watch the light to-day, that we may not give them a dark drive to-morrow.

They send their best love to papa and everybody, with George's thanks for the letter brought by this post. Martha begs my brother may be assured of her interest in everything relating to him and his family, and of her sincerely partaking our pleasure in the receipt of every good account from Godmersham.

Of Chawton I think I can have nothing more to say, but that everything you say about it in the letter now before me will, I am sure, as soon as I am able to read it to her, make my mother consider the plan with more and more pleasure. We had formed the same views on H. Digweed's farm.

A very kind and feeling letter is arrived to-day from Kintbury. Mrs. Fowle's sympathy and solicitude on such an occasion you will be able to do justice to, and to express it as she wishes to my brother. Concerning you, she says: "Cassandra will, I know, excuse my writing to her; it is not to save myself but her that I omit so doing. Give my best, my kindest love to her, and tell her I feel for her as I know she would for me on the same occasion, and that I most sincerely hope her health will not suffer."

We have just had two hampers of apples from Kintbury, and the floor of our little garret is almost covered. Love to all.

Yours very affectionately,
J. A.

Miss AUSTEN, EDWARD AUSTEN'S, Esq.,
Godmersham Park, Faversham, Kent.

XXVIII.

CASTLE SQUARE, Sunday (November 21).

YOUR letter, my dear Cassandra, obliges me to write immediately, that you may have the earliest notice of Frank's intending, if possible, to go to Godmersham exactly at the time now fixed for your visit to Goodnestone.

He resolved, almost directly on the receipt of your former letter, to try for an extension of his leave of absence, that he might be able to go down to you for two days, but charged me not to give you any notice of it, on account of the uncertainty of success. Now, however, I must give it, and now perhaps he may be giving it himself; for I am just in the hateful predicament of being obliged to write what I know will somehow or other be of no use.

He meant to ask for five days more, and if they were granted, to go down by Thursday night's mail, and spend Friday and Saturday with you; and he considered his chance of succeeding by no means bad. I hope it will take place as he planned, and that your arrangements with Goodnestone may admit of suitable alteration.

Your news of Edward Bridges was quite news, for I have had no letter from Wrotham. I wish him happy with all my heart, and hope his choice may turn out according to his own expectations, and beyond those of his family; and I dare say it will. Marriage is a great improver, and in a similar situation Harriet may be as amiable as Eleanor. As to money, that will come, you may be sure, because they cannot do without it. When you see him again, pray give him our congratulations and best wishes. This match will certainly set John and Lucy going.

There are six bedchambers at Chawton; Henry wrote to my mother the other day, and luckily mentioned the number, which is just what we wanted to be assured of. He speaks also of garrets for store-places, one of which she immediately planned fitting up for Edward's man-servant; and now perhaps it must be for our own; for she is already quite reconciled to our keeping one. The difficulty of doing without one had been thought of before. His name shall be Robert, if you please.

Before I can tell you of it, you will have heard that Miss Sawbridge is married. It took place, I believe, on Thursday. Mrs. Fowle has for some time been in the secret, but the neighborhood in general were quite unsuspicious. Mr. Maxwell was tutor to the young Gregorys,—consequently, they must be one of the happiest couples in the world, and either of them worthy of envy, for she must be excessively in love, and he mounts from nothing to a comfortable home. Martha has heard him very highly spoken of. They continue for the present at Speen Hill.

I have a Southampton match to return for your Kentish one, Captain G. Heathcote and Miss A. Lyell. I have it from Alethea, and like it, because I had made it before.

Yes, the Stoneleigh business is concluded, but it was not till yesterday that my mother was regularly informed of it, though the news had reached us on Monday evening by way of Steventon. My aunt says as little as may be on the subject by way of information, and nothing at all by way of satisfaction. She reflects on Mr. T. Leigh's dilatoriness, and looks about with great diligence and success for inconvenience and evil, among which she ingeniously places the danger of her new housemaids catching cold on the outside of the coach, when she goes down to Bath, for a carriage makes her sick.

John Binns has been offered their place, but declines it; as she supposes, because he will not wear a livery. Whatever be the cause, I like the effect.

In spite of all my mother's long and intimate knowledge of the writer, she was not up to the expectation of such a letter as this; the discontentedness of it shocked and surprised her—but I see nothing in it out of nature, though a sad nature.

She does not forget to wish for Chambers, you may be sure. No particulars are given, not a word of arrears mentioned, though in her letter to James they were in a general way spoken of. The amount of them is a matter of conjecture, and to my mother a most interesting one; she cannot fix any time for their beginning with any satisfaction to herself but Mrs. Leigh's death, and Henry's two thousand pounds neither agrees with that period nor any other. I did not like to own our previous information of what was intended last July, and have therefore only said that if we could see Henry we might hear many particulars, as I had understood that some confidential conversation had passed between him and Mr. T. L. at Stoneleigh.

We have been as quiet as usual since Frank and Mary left us; Mr. Criswick called on Martha that very morning on his way home again from Portsmouth, and we have had no visitor since.

We called on the Miss Lyells one day, and heard a good account of Mr. Heathcote's canvass, the success of which, of course, exceeds his expectations. Alethea in her letter hopes for my interest, which I conclude means Edward's, and I take this opportunity, therefore, of requesting that he will bring in Mr. Heathcote. Mr. Lane told us yesterday that Mr. H. had behaved very handsomely, and waited on Mr. Thistlethwaite, to say that if he (Mr. T.) would stand, he (Mr. H.) would not oppose him; but Mr. T. declined it, acknowledging himself still smarting under the payment of late electioneering costs.

The Mrs. Hulberts, we learn from Kintbury, come to Steventon this week, and bring Mary Jane Fowle with them on her way to Mrs. Nune's; she returns at Christmas with her brother.

Our brother we may perhaps see in the course of a few days, and we mean to take the opportunity of his help to go one night to the play. Martha ought to see the inside of the theatre once while she lives in Southampton, and I think she will hardly wish to take a second view.

The furniture of Bellevue is to be sold to-morrow, and we shall take it in our usual walk, if the weather be favorable.

How could you have a wet day on Thursday? With us it was a prince of days, the most delightful we have had for weeks; soft, bright, with a brisk wind from the southwest; everybody was out and talking of spring, and Martha and I did not know how to turn back. On Friday evening we had some very blowing weather,—from six to nine; I think we never heard it worse, even here. And one night we had so much rain that it forced its way again into the store-closet; and though the evil was comparatively slight and the mischief nothing, I had some employment the next day in drying parcels, etc. I have now moved still more out of the way.

Martha sends her best love, and thanks you for admitting her to the knowledge of the pros and cons about Harriet Foote; she has an interest in all such matters. I am also to say that she wants to see you. Mary Jane missed her papa and mamma a good deal at first, but now does very well without them. I am glad to hear of little John's being better, and hope your accounts of Mrs. Knight will also improve. Adieu! remember me affectionately to everybody, and believe me,

Ever yours,
J. A.

Miss AUSTEN, EDWARD AUSTEN'S, Esq.,
Godmersham Park, Faversham, Kent.

XXIX.

CASTLE SQUARE, Friday (December 9).

MANY thanks, my dear Cassandra, to you and Mr. Deedes for your joint and agreeable composition, which took me by surprise this morning. He has certainly great merit as a writer; he does ample justice to his subject, and without being diffuse is clear and correct; and though I do not mean to compare his epistolary powers with yours, or to give him the same portion of my gratitude, he certainly has a very pleasing way of winding up a whole, and speeding truth into the world.

"But all this," as my dear Mrs. Piozzi says, "is flight and fancy and nonsense, for my master has his great casks to mind and I have my little children." It is you, however, in this instance, that have the little children, and I that have the great cask, for we are brewing spruce beer again; but my meaning really is, that I am extremely foolish in writing all this unnecessary stuff when I have so many matters to write about that my paper will hardly hold it all. Little matters they are, to be sure, but highly important.

In the first place, Miss Curling is actually at Portsmouth, which I was always in hopes would not happen. I wish her no worse, however, than a long and happy abode there. Here she would probably be dull, and I am sure she would be troublesome.

The bracelets are in my possession, and everything I could wish them to be. They came with Martha's pelisse, which likewise gives great satisfaction.

Soon after I had closed my last letter to you we were visited by Mrs. Dickens and her sister-in-law, Mrs. Bertie, the wife of a lately made Admiral. Mrs. F. A.,[8] I believe, was their first object, but they put up with us very kindly, and Mrs. D., finding in Miss Lloyd a friend of Mrs. Dundas, had another motive for the acquaintance. She seems a really agreeable woman,—that is, her manners are gentle, and she knows a great many of our connections in West Kent. Mrs. Bertie lives in the Polygon, and was out when we returned her visit, which are her two virtues.

A larger circle of acquaintance, and an increase of amusement, is quite in character with our approaching removal. Yes, I mean to go to as many balls as possible, that I may have a good bargain. Everybody is very much concerned at our going away, and everybody is acquainted with Chawton, and speaks of it as a remarkably pretty village, and everybody knows the house we describe, but nobody fixes on the right.

I am very much obliged to Mrs. Knight for such a proof of the interest she takes in me, and she may depend upon it that I will marry Mr. Papillon, whatever may be his reluctance or my own. I owe her much more than such a trifling sacrifice.

Our ball was rather more amusing than I expected. Martha liked it very much, and I did not gape till the last quarter of an hour. It was past nine before we were sent for, and not twelve when we returned. The room was tolerably full, and there were, perhaps, thirty couple of dancers. The melancholy part was to see so many dozen young women standing by without partners, and each of them with two ugly naked shoulders.

It was the same room in which we danced fifteen years ago. I thought it all over, and in spite of the shame of being so much older, felt with thankfulness that I was quite as happy now as then. We paid an additional shilling for our tea, which we took as we chose in an adjoining and very comfortable room.

There were only four dances, and it went to my heart that the Miss Lances (one of them, too, named Emma) should have partners only for two. You will not expect to hear that I was asked to dance, but I was—by the gentleman whom we met that Sunday with Captain D'Auvergne. We have always kept up a bowing acquaintance since, and, being pleased with his black eyes, I spoke to him at the ball, which brought on me this civility; but I do not know his name, and he seems so little at home in the English language that I believe his black eyes may be the best of him. Captain D'Auvergne has got a ship.

Martha and I made use of the very favorable state of yesterday for walking, to pay our duty at Chiswell. We found Mrs. Lance at home and alone, and sat out three other ladies who soon came in. We went by the ferry, and returned by the bridge, and were scarcely at all fatigued.

Edward must have enjoyed the last two days. You, I presume, had a cool drive to Canterbury. Kitty Foote came on Wednesday; and her evening visit began early enough for the last part, the apple-pie, of our dinner, for we never dine now till five.

Yesterday I—or rather, you—had a letter from Nanny Hilliard, the object of which is that she would be very much obliged to us if we would get Hannah a place. I am sorry that I cannot assist her; if you can, let me know, as I shall not answer the letter immediately. Mr. Sloper is married again, not much to Nanny's, or anybody's satisfaction. The lady was governess to Sir Robert's natural children, and seems to have nothing to recommend her. I do not find, however, that Nanny is likely to lose her place in consequence. She says not a word of what service she wishes for Hannah, or what Hannah can do; but a nursery, I suppose, or something of that kind, must be the thing.

Having now cleared away my smaller articles of news, I come to a communication of some weight; no less than that my uncle and aunt[9] are going to allow James 100*l.* a year. We hear of it through Steventon. Mary sent us the other day an extract from my aunt's letter on the subject, in which the donation is made with the greatest kindness, and intended as a compensation for his loss in the conscientious refusal of Hampstead living; 100*l.* a year being all that he had at the time called its worth, as I find it was always intended at Steventon to divide the real income with Kintbury.

Nothing can be more affectionate than my aunt's language in

making the present, and likewise in expressing her hope of their being much more together in future than, to her great regret, they have of late years been. My expectations for my mother do not rise with this event. We will allow a little more time, however, before we fly out.

If not prevented by parish business, James comes to us on Monday. The Mrs. Hulberts and Miss Murden are their guests at present, and likely to continue such till Christmas. Anna comes home on the 19th. The hundred a year begins next Lady-day.

I am glad you are to have Henry with you again; with him and the boys you cannot but have a cheerful, and at times even a merry, Christmas. Martha is so [*MSS. torn*]. . . . We want to be settled at Chawton in time for Henry to come to us for some shooting in October, at least, or a little earlier, and Edward may visit us after taking his boys back to Winchester. Suppose we name the 4th of September. Will not that do?

I have but one thing more to tell you. Mrs. Hill called on my mother yesterday while we were gone to Chiswell, and in the course of the visit asked her whether she knew anything of a clergyman's family of the name of Alford, who had resided in our part of Hampshire. Mrs. Hill had been applied to as likely to give some information of them on account of their probable vicinity to Dr. Hill's living by a lady, or for a lady, who had known Mrs. and the two Miss Alfords in Bath, whither they had removed it seems from Hampshire, and who now wishes to convey to the Miss Alfords some work or trimming which she has been doing for them; but the mother and daughters have left Bath, and the lady cannot learn where they are gone to. While my mother gave us the account, the probability of its being ourselves occurred to us, and it had previously struck herself ... what makes it more likely, and even indispensably to be us, is that she mentioned Mr. Hammond as now having the living or curacy which the father had had. I cannot think who our kind lady can be, but I dare say we shall not like the work.

Distribute the affectionate love of a heart not so tired as the right hand belonging to it.

Yours ever sincerely,
J. A.

Miss AUSTEN, EDWARD AUSTEN'S, Esq.,
Godmersham Park, Faversham, Kent.

FOOTNOTES:

[8] Frank Austen.
[9] Mr. and Mrs. Leigh Perrot.

XXX.

***

CASTLE SQUARE, Tuesday (December 27).

MY DEAR CASSANDRA,—I can now write at leisure and make the most of my subjects, which is lucky, as they are not numerous this week.

Our house was cleared by half-past eleven on Saturday, and we had the satisfaction of hearing yesterday that the party reached home in safety soon after five.

I was very glad of your letter this morning; for, my mother taking medicine, Eliza keeping her bed with a cold, and Choles not coming, made us rather dull and dependent on the post. You tell me much that gives me pleasure, but I think not much to answer. I wish I could help you in your needlework. I have two hands and a new thimble that lead a very easy life.

Lady Sondes' match surprises, but does not offend me; had her first marriage been of affection, or had there been a grown-up single daughter, I should not have forgiven her; but I consider everybody as having a right to marry once in their lives for love, if they can, and provided she will now leave off having bad headaches and being pathetic, I can allow her, I can wish her, to be happy.

Do not imagine that your picture of your *tête-à-tête* with Sir B. makes any change in our expectations here; he could not be really reading, though he held the newspaper in his hand; he was making up his mind to the deed, and the manner of it. I think you will have a letter from him soon.

I heard from Portsmouth yesterday, and as I am to send them more clothes, they cannot be expecting a very early return to us.

Mary's face is pretty well, but she must have suffered a great deal with it; an abscess was formed and opened.

Our evening party on Thursday produced nothing more remarkable than Miss Murden's coming too, though she had declined it absolutely in the morning, and sitting very ungracious and very silent with us from seven o'clock till half after eleven, for so late was it, owing to the chairmen, before we got rid of them.

The last hour, spent in yawning and shivering in a wide circle round the fire, was dull enough, but the tray had admirable success. The widgeon and the preserved ginger were as delicious as one could wish. But as to our black butter, do not decoy anybody to Southampton by such a lure, for it is all gone. The first pot was opened when Frank and Mary were here, and proved not at all what it ought to be; it was neither solid nor entirely sweet, and on seeing it, Eliza remembered that Miss Austen had said she did not think it had been boiled enough. It was made, you know, when we were absent. Such being the event of the first pot, I would not save the second, and we therefore ate it in unpretending privacy; and though not what it ought to be, part of it was very good.

James means to keep three horses on this increase of income; at present he has but one. Mary wishes the other two to be fit to carry women, and in the purchase of one Edward will probably be called upon to fulfil his promise to his godson. We have now pretty well ascertained James's income to be eleven hundred pounds, curate paid, which makes us very happy,—the ascertainment as well as the income.

Mary does not talk of the garden; it may well be a disagreeable subject to her, but her husband is persuaded that nothing is wanting to make the first new one good but trenching, which is to be done by his own servants and John Bond, by degrees, not at the expense which trenching the other amounted to.

I was happy to hear, chiefly for Anna's sake, that a ball at Manydown was once more in agitation; it is called a child's ball, and given by Mrs. Heathcote to Wm. Such was its beginning at least, but it will probably swell into something more. Edward was invited during his stay at Manydown, and it is to take place between this and Twelfth-day. Mrs. Hulbert has taken Anna a pair of white shoes on the occasion.

I forgot in my last to tell you that we hear, by way of Kintbury and the Palmers, that they were all well at Bermuda in the beginning of Nov.

Wednesday.—Yesterday must have been a day of sad remembrance at Gm.[10] I am glad it is over. We spent Friday evening with our friends at the boarding-house, and our curiosity was gratified by the sight of their fellow-inmates, Mrs. Drew and Miss Hook, Mr. Wynne and Mr. Fitzhugh; the latter is brother to Mrs. Lance, and very much the gentleman. He has lived in that house more than twenty years, and, poor man! is so totally deaf that they say he could not hear a cannon, were it fired close to him; having no cannon at hand to make the experiment, I took it for granted, and talked to him a little with my fingers, which was funny enough. I recommended him to read "Corinna."

Miss Hook is a well-behaved, genteelish woman; Mrs. Drew well behaved, without being at all genteel. Mr. Wynne seems a chatty and rather familiar young man. Miss Murden was quite a different creature this last evening from what she had been before, owing to her having with Martha's help found a situation in the morning, which bids very fair for comfort. When she leaves Steventon, she comes to board and lodge with Mrs. Hookey, the chemist—for there is no Mr. Hookey. I cannot say that I am in any hurry for the conclusion of her present visit, but I was truly glad to see her comfortable in mind and spirits; at her age, perhaps, one may be as friendless oneself, and in similar circumstances quite as captious.

My mother has been lately adding to her possessions in plate,—a whole tablespoon and a whole dessert-spoon, and six whole teaspoons,—which makes our sideboard border on the magnificent. They were mostly the produce of old or useless silver. I have turned the 11*s*. in the list into 12*s*., and the card looks all the better; a silver tea-ladle is also added, which will at least answer the purpose of making us sometimes think of John Warren.

I have laid Lady Sondes' case before Martha, who does not make the least objection to it, and is particularly pleased with the name of Montresor. I do not agree with her there, but I like his rank very much, and always affix the ideas of strong sense and highly elegant manners to a general.

I must write to Charles next week. You may guess in what extravagant terms of praise Earle Harwood speaks of him. He is looked up to by everybody in all America.

I shall not tell you anything more of Wm. Digweed's china, as your silence on the subject makes you unworthy of it. Mrs. H. Digweed looks forward with great satisfaction to our being her neighbors. I would have her enjoy the idea to the utmost, as I suspect there will not be much in the reality. With equal pleasure we anticipate an intimacy with her husband's bailiff and his wife, who live close by us, and are said to be remarkably good sort of people.

Yes, yes, we will have a pianoforte, as good a one as can be got for thirty guineas, and I will practise country dances, that we may have some amusement for our nephews and nieces, when we have the pleasure of their company.

Martha sends her love to Henry, and tells him that he will soon have a bill of Miss Chaplin's, about 14*l*., to pay on her account; but the bill shall not be sent in till his return to town. I hope he comes to you in good health, and in spirits as good as a first return to Godmersham can allow. With his nephews he will force himself to be cheerful, till he really is so. Send me some intelligence of Eliza; it is a long while since I have heard of her.

We have had snow on the ground here almost a week; it is now going, but Southampton must boast no longer. We all send our love to Edward junior and his brothers, and I hope Speculation is generally liked.

Fare you well.

Yours affectionately,
J. AUSTEN.

My mother has not been out of doors this week, but she keeps pretty well. We have received through Bookham an indifferent account of your godmother.

Miss AUSTEN, EDWARD AUSTEN'S, Esq.,
Godmersham Park, Faversham, Kent.

FOOTNOTES:

[10] Godmersham, Edward Austen's place.

XXXI.

CASTLE SQUARE, Tuesday (January 10, 1809).

I AM not surprised, my dear Cassandra, that you did not find my last letter very full of matter, and I wish this may not have the same deficiency; but we are doing nothing ourselves to write about, and I am therefore quite dependent upon the communications of our friends, or my own wits.

This post brought me two interesting letters, yours and one from Bookham, in answer to an inquiry of mine about your good godmother, of whom we had lately received a very alarming account from Paragon. Miss Arnold was the informant then, and she spoke of Mrs. E. L. having been very dangerously ill, and attended by a physician from Oxford.

Your letter to Adlestrop may perhaps bring you information from the spot, but in case it should not, I must tell you that she is better; though Dr. Bourne cannot yet call her out of danger; such was the case last Wednesday, and Mrs. Cooke's having had no later account is a favorable sign. I am to hear again from the latter next week, but not this, if everything goes on well.

Her disorder is an inflammation on the lungs, arising from a severe chill taken in church last Sunday three weeks; her mind all pious composure, as may be supposed. George Cooke was there when her illness began; his brother has now taken his place. Her age and feebleness considered, one's fears cannot but preponderate, though her amendment has already surpassed the expectation of the physician at the beginning. I am sorry to add that Becky is laid up with a complaint of the same kind.

I am very glad to have the time of your return at all fixed;

we all rejoice in it, and it will not be later than I had expected. I dare not hope that Mary and Miss Curling may be detained at Portsmouth so long or half so long; but it would be worth twopence to have it so.

The "St. Albans" perhaps may soon be off to help bring home what may remain by this time of our poor army, whose state seems dreadfully critical. The "Regency" seems to have been heard of only here; my most political correspondents make no mention of it. Unlucky that I should have wasted so much reflection on the subject.

I can now answer your question to my mother more at large, and likewise more at small—with equal perspicuity and minuteness; for the very day of our leaving Southampton is fixed; and if the knowledge is of no use to Edward, I am sure it will give him pleasure. Easter Monday, April 3, is the day; we are to sleep that night at Alton, and be with our friends at Bookham the next, if they are then at home; there we remain till the following Monday, and on Tuesday, April 11, hope to be at Godmersham. If the Cookes are absent, we shall finish our journey on the 5th. These plans depend of course upon the weather, but I hope there will be no settled cold to delay us materially.

To make you amends for being at Bookham, it is in contemplation to spend a few days at Baiton Lodge in our way out of Kent. The hint of such a visit is most affectionately welcomed by Mrs. Birch, in one of her odd pleasant letters lately, in which she speaks of us with the usual distinguished kindness, declaring that she shall not be at all satisfied unless a very handsome present is made us immediately from one quarter.

Fanny's not coming with you is no more than we expected; and as we have not the hope of a bed for her, and shall see her so soon afterwards at Godmersham, we cannot wish it otherwise.

William will be quite recovered, I trust, by the time you receive this. What a comfort his cross-stitch must have been! Pray tell him that I should like to see his work very much. I hope our answers this morning have given satisfaction; we had great pleasure in Uncle Deedes' packet; and pray let Marianne know, in private, that I think she is quite right to work a rug for Uncle John's coffee urn, and that I am sure it must give great pleasure to herself now, and to him when he receives it.

The preference of Brag over Speculation does not greatly surprise me, I believe, because I feel the same myself; but it mortifies me deeply, because Speculation was under my patronage; and, after all, what is there so delightful in a pair royal of Braggers? It is but three nines or three knaves, or a mixture of them. When one comes to reason upon it, it cannot stand its ground against Speculation,—of which I hope Edward is now convinced. Give my love to him if he is.

The letter from Paragon before mentioned was much like those which had preceded it, as to the felicity of its writer. They found their house so dirty and so damp that they were obliged to be a week at an inn. John Binns had behaved most unhandsomely, and engaged himself elsewhere. They have a man, however, on the same footing, which my aunt does not like, and she finds both him and the new maid-servant very, very inferior to Robert and Martha. Whether they mean to have any other domestics does not appear, nor whether they are to have a carriage while they are in Bath.

The Holders are as usual, though I believe it is not very usual for them to be happy, which they now are at a great rate, in Hooper's marriage. The Irvines are not mentioned. The American lady improved as we went on; but still the same faults in part recurred.

We are now in Margiana, and like it very well indeed. We are just going to set off for Northumberland to be shut up in Widdrington Tower, where there must be two or three sets of victims already immured under a very fine villain.

Wednesday.—Your report of Eliza's health gives me great pleasure, and the progress of the bank is a constant source of satisfaction. With such increasing profits, tell Henry that I hope he will not work poor High-Diddle so hard as he used to do.

Has your newspaper given a sad story of a Mrs. Middleton, wife of a farmer in Yorkshire, her sister, and servant, being almost frozen to death in the late weather, her little child quite so? I hope the sister is not our friend Miss Woodd, and I rather think her brother-in-law had moved into Lincolnshire, but their name and station accord too well. Mrs. M. and the maid are said to be tolerably recovered, but the sister is likely to lose the use of her limbs.

Charles's rug will be finished to-day, and sent to-morrow to Frank, to be consigned by him to Mr. Turner's care; and I am going to send Marmion out with it,—very generous in me, I think.

As we have no letter from Adlestrop, we may suppose the good woman was alive on Monday, but I cannot help expecting bad news from thence or Bookham in a few days. Do you continue quite well?

Have you nothing to say of your little namesake? We join in love and many happy returns.

Yours affectionately,
J. AUSTEN.

The Manydown ball was a smaller thing than I expected, but it seems to have made Anna very happy. At her age it would not have done for me.

Miss AUSTEN, EDWARD AUSTEN'S, Esq.,
Godmersham Park, Faversham, Kent.

XXXII.

CASTLE SQUARE, Tuesday (January 17).

MY DEAR CASSANDRA,—I am happy to say that we had no second letter from Bookham last week. Yours has brought its usual measure of satisfaction and amusement, and I beg your acceptance of all the thanks due on the occasion. Your offer of cravats is very kind, and happens to be particularly adapted to my wants, but it was an odd thing to occur to you.

Yes, we have got another fall of snow, and are very dreadful; everything seems to turn to snow this winter.

I hope you have had no more illness among you, and that William will be soon as well as ever. His working a footstool for Chawton is a most agreeable surprise to me, and I am sure his grandmamma will value it very much as a proof of his affection and industry, but we shall never have the heart to put our feet upon it. I believe I must work a muslin cover in satin stitch to keep it from the dirt. I long to know what his colors are. I guess greens and purples.

Edward and Henry have started a difficulty respecting our journey, which, I must own with some confusion, had never been thought of by us; but if the former expected by it to prevent our travelling into Kent entirely, he will be disappointed, for we have already determined to go the Croydon road on leaving Bookham and sleep at Dartford. Will not that do? There certainly does seem no convenient resting-place on the other road.

Anna went to Clanville last Friday, and I have hopes of her new aunt's being really worth her knowing. Perhaps you may never have heard that James and Mary paid a morning visit there in form some weeks ago, and Mary, though by no means disposed to like her, was very much pleased with her indeed. Her praise, to be sure, proves nothing more than Mrs. M.'s being civil and attentive to them, but her being so is in favor of her having good sense. Mary writes of Anna as improved in person, but gives her no other commendation. I am afraid her absence now may deprive her of one pleasure, for that silly Mr. Hammond is actually to give his ball on Friday.

We had some reason to expect a visit from Earle Harwood and James this week, but they do not come. Miss Murden arrived last night at Mrs. Hookey's, as a message and a basket announced to us. You will therefore return to an enlarged and, of course, improved society here, especially as the Miss Williamses are come back.

We were agreeably surprised the other day by a visit from your beauty and mine, each in a new cloth mantle and bonnet; and I dare say you will value yourself much on the modest propriety of Miss W.'s taste, hers being purple and Miss Grace's scarlet.

I can easily suppose that your six weeks here will be fully occupied, were it only in lengthening the waists of your gowns. I have pretty well arranged my spring and summer plans of that kind, and mean to wear out my spotted muslin before I go. You will exclaim at this, but mine really has signs of feebleness, which with a little care may come to something.

Martha and Dr. Mant are as bad as ever; he runs after her in the street to apologize for having spoken to a gentleman while she was near him the day before. Poor Mrs. Mant can stand it no longer; she is retired to one of her married daughters'.

When William returns to Winchester Mary Jane is to go to Mrs. Nune's for a month, and then to Steventon for a fortnight, and it seems likely that she and her aunt Martha may travel into Berkshire together.

We shall not have a month of Martha after your return, and that month will be a very interrupted and broken one, but we shall enjoy ourselves the more when we can get a quiet half-hour together.

To set against your new novel, of which nobody ever heard before, and perhaps never may again, we have got "Ida of Athens," by Miss Owenson, which must be very clever, because it was written, as the authoress says, in three months. We have only read the preface yet, but her Irish girl does not make me expect much. If the warmth of her language could affect the body, it might be worth reading in this weather.

Adieu! I must leave off to stir the fire and call on Miss Murden.

Evening.—I have done them both, the first very often. We found our friend as comfortable as she can ever allow herself to be in cold weather. There is a very neat parlor behind the shop for her to sit in, not very light indeed, being *à la* Southampton, the middle of three deep, but very lively from the frequent sound of the pestle and mortar.

We afterwards called on the Miss Williamses, who lodge at Durantoy's. Miss Mary only was at home, and she is in very indifferent health. Dr. Hacket came in while we were there, and said that he never remembered such a severe winter as this in Southampton before. It is bad, but we do not suffer as we did last year, because the wind has been more N.E. than N.W.

For a day or two last week my mother was very poorly with a return of one of her old complaints, but it did not last long, and seems to have left nothing bad behind it. She began to talk of a serious illness, her two last having been preceded by the same symptoms, but, thank heaven! she is now quite as well as one can expect her to be in weather which deprives her of exercise.

Miss M. conveys to us a third volume of sermons, from Hamstall, just published, and which we are to like better than the two others; they are professedly practical, and for the use of country congregations. I have just received some verses in an unknown hand, and am desired to forward them to my nephew Edward at Godmersham.

Alas! poor Brag, thou boastful game!
What now avails thine empty name?
Where now thy more distinguished fame?
My day is o'er, and thine the same,
For thou, like me, art thrown aside
At Godmersham, this Christmastide;
And now across the table wide
Each game save brag or spec. is tried.
Such is the mild ejaculation
Of tender-hearted speculation.

Wednesday.—I expected to have a letter from somebody to-day, but I have not. Twice every day I think of a letter from Portsmouth.

Miss Murden has been sitting with us this morning. As yet she seems very well pleased with her situation. The worst part of her being in Southampton will be the necessity of one walking with her now and then, for she talks so loud that one is quite ashamed; but our dining hours are luckily very different, which we shall take all reasonable advantage of.

The Queen's birthday moves the assembly to this night instead of last, and as it is always fully attended, Martha and I expect an amusing show. We were in hopes of being independent of other companions by having the attendance of Mr. Austen and Captain Harwood; but as they fail us, we are obliged to look out for other help, and have fixed on the Wallops as least likely to be troublesome. I have called on them this morning and found them very willing, and I am sorry that you must wait a whole week for the particulars of the evening. I propose being asked to dance by our acquaintance Mr. Smith, now *Captain* Smith, who has lately reappeared in Southampton, but I shall decline it. He saw Charles last August.

What an alarming bride Mrs. —— must have been; such a parade is one of the most immodest pieces of modesty that one can imagine. To attract notice could have been her only wish.

It augurs ill for her family; it announces not great sense, and therefore insures boundless influence.

I hope Fanny's visit is now taking place. You have said scarcely anything of her lately, but I trust you are as good friends as ever.

Martha sends her love, and hopes to have the pleasure of seeing you when you return to Southampton. You are to understand this message as being merely for the sake of a message to oblige me.

Yours affectionately,
J. AUSTEN.

Henry never sent his love to me in your last, but I send him mine.

Miss AUSTEN, EDWARD AUSTEN'S, Esq.,
Godmersham Park, Faversham, Kent.

XXXIII.

CASTLE SQUARE, Tuesday (January 24).

MY DEAR CASSANDRA,—I will give you the indulgence of a letter on Thursday this week, instead of Friday, but I do not require you to write again before Sunday, provided I may believe you and your finger going on quite well. Take care of your precious self; do not work too hard. Remember that Aunt Cassandras are quite as scarce as Miss Beverleys.[11]

I had the happiness yesterday of a letter from Charles, but I shall say as little about it as possible, because I know that excruciating Henry will have had a letter likewise, to make all my intelligence valueless. It was written at Bermuda on the 7th and 10th of December. All well, and Fanny still only in expectation of being otherwise. He had taken a small prize in his late cruise,—a French schooner, laden with sugar; but bad weather parted them, and she had not yet been heard of. His cruise ended December 1st. My September letter was the latest he had received.

This day three weeks you are to be in London, and I wish you better weather; not but that you may have worse, for we have now nothing but ceaseless snow or rain and insufferable dirt to complain of; no tempestuous winds nor severity of cold. Since I wrote last we have had something of each, but it is not genteel to rip up old grievances.

You used me scandalously by not mentioning Edward Cooper's sermons. I tell you everything, and it is unknown the mysteries you conceal from me; and, to add to the rest, you persevere in giving a final "e" to "invalid," thereby putting it out of one's power to suppose Mrs. E. Leigh, even for a moment, a veteran soldier.

She, good woman, is, I hope, destined for some further placid enjoyment of her own excellence in this world, for her recovery advances exceedingly well.

I had this pleasant news in a letter from Bookham last Thursday; but as the letter was from Mary instead of her mother, you will guess her account was not equally good from home. Mrs. Cooke had been confined to her bed some days by illness, but was then better, and Mary wrote in confidence of her continuing to mend. I have desired to hear again soon.

You rejoice me by what you say of Fanny.[12] I hope she will not turn good-for-nothing this ever so long. We thought of and talked of her yesterday with sincere affection, and wished her a long enjoyment of all the happiness to which she seems born. While she gives happiness to those about her she is pretty sure of her own share.

I am gratified by her having pleasure in what I write, but I wish the knowledge of my being exposed to her discerning criticism may not hurt my style, by inducing too great a solicitude. I begin already to weigh my words and sentences more than I did, and am looking about for a sentiment, an illustration, or a metaphor in every corner of the room. Could my ideas flow as fast as the rain in the store-closet, it would be charming.

We have been in two or three dreadful states within the last week, from the melting of the snow, etc., and the contest between us and the closet has now ended in our defeat. I have been obliged to move almost everything out of it, and leave it to splash itself as it likes.

You have by no means raised my curiosity after Caleb. My disinclination for it before was affected, but now it is real. I do not like the evangelicals. Of course I shall be delighted when I read it, like other people; but till I do I dislike it.

I am sorry my verses did not bring any return from Edward. I was in hopes they might, but I suppose he does not rate them high enough. It might be partiality, but they seemed to me purely classical,—just like Homer and Virgil, Ovid and Propria que Maribus.

I had a nice brotherly letter from Frank the other day, which, after an interval of nearly three weeks, was very welcome. No orders were come on Friday, and none were come yesterday, or we should have heard to-day. I had supposed Miss C. would share her cousin's room here, but a message in this letter proves the contrary. I will make the garret as comfortable as I can, but the possibilities of that apartment are not great.

My mother has been talking to Eliza about our future home, and she, making no difficulty at all of the sweetheart, is perfectly disposed to continue with us, but till she has written home for mother's approbation cannot quite decide. Mother does not like to have her so far off. At Chawton she will be nine or ten miles nearer, which I hope will have its due influence.

As for Sally, she means to play John Binns with us, in her anxiety to belong to our household again. Hitherto she appears a very good servant.

You depend upon finding all your plants dead, I hope. They look very ill, I understand.

Your silence on the subject of our ball makes me suppose your curiosity too great for words. We were very well entertained, and could have stayed longer but for the arrival of my list shoes to convey me home, and I did not like to keep them waiting in the cold. The room was tolerably full, and the ball opened by Miss Glyn. The Miss Lances had partners, Captain Dauvergne's friend appeared in regimentals, Caroline Maitland had an officer to flirt with, and Mr. John Harrison was deputed by Captain Smith, being himself absent, to ask me to dance. Everything went well, you see, especially after we had tucked Mrs. Lance's neckerchief in behind and fastened it with a pin.

We had a very full and agreeable account of Mr. Hammond's ball from Anna last night; the same fluent pen has sent similar information, I know, into Kent. She seems to have been as happy as one could wish her, and the complacency of her mamma in doing the honors of the evening must have made her pleasure almost as great. The grandeur of the meeting was beyond my hopes. I should like to have seen Anna's looks and performance, but that sad cropped head must have injured the former.

Martha pleases herself with believing that if I had kept her counsel you would never have heard of Dr. M.'s late behavior, as if the very slight manner in which I mentioned it could have been all on which you found your judgment. I do not endeavor to undeceive her, because I wish her happy, at all events, and know how highly she prizes happiness of any kind. She is, moreover, so full of kindness for us both, and sends you in particular so many good wishes about your finger, that I am willing to overlook a venial fault, and as Dr. M. is a clergyman, their attachment, however immoral, has a decorous air. Adieu, sweet You. This is grievous news from Spain. It is well that Dr. Moore was spared the knowledge of such a son's death.

Yours affectionately,
J. AUSTEN.

Anna's hand gets better and better; it begins to be too good for any consequence.

We send best love to dear little Lizzy and Marianne in particular.

The Portsmouth paper gave a melancholy history of a poor mad woman, escaped from confinement, who said her husband and daughter, of the name of Payne, lived at Ashford, in Kent. Do you own them?

Miss AUSTEN, EDWARD AUSTEN'S, Esq.,
Godmersham Park, Faversham, Kent.

FOOTNOTES:

[11] "Cecilia" Beverley, the heroine of Miss Burney's novel.

[12] Fanny Austen, afterward Lady Edward Knatchbull.

XXXIV.

CASTLE SQUARE, Monday (January 30).

MY DEAR CASSANDRA,—I was not much surprised yesterday by the agreeable surprise of your letter, and extremely glad to receive the assurance of your finger being well again.

Here is such a wet day as never was seen. I wish the poor little girls had better weather for their journey; they must amuse themselves with watching the raindrops down the windows. Sackree, I suppose, feels quite broken-hearted. I cannot have done with the weather without observing how delightfully mild it is; I am sure Fanny must enjoy it with us. Yesterday was a very blowing day; we got to church, however, which we had not been able to do for two Sundays before.

I am not at all ashamed about the name of the novel, having been guilty of no insult toward your handwriting; the diphthong I always saw, but knowing how fond you were of adding a vowel wherever you could, I attributed it to that alone, and the knowledge of the truth does the book no service; the only merit it could have was in the name of Caleb, which has an honest, unpretending sound, but in C[oe]lebs there is pedantry and affectation. Is it written only to classical scholars?

I shall now try to say only what is necessary, I am weary of meandering; so expect a vast deal of small matter, concisely told, in the next two pages.

Mrs. Cooke has been very dangerously ill, but is now, I hope, safe. I had a letter last week from George, Mary being too busy to write, and at that time the disorder was called of the typhus kind, and their alarm considerable, but yesterday brought me a much better account from Mary, the origin of the complaint being now ascertained to be bilious, and the strong medicines requisite promising to be effectual. Mrs. E. L. is so muchrecovered as to get into the dressing-room every day.

A letter from Hamstall gives us the history of Sir Tho. Williams's return. The Admiral, whoever he might he, took a fancy to the "Neptune," and having only a worn-out 74 to offer in lieu of it, Sir Tho. declined such a command, and is come home passenger. Lucky man! to have so fair an opportunity of escape. I hope his wife allows herself to be happy on the occasion, and does not give all her thoughts to being nervous.

A great event happens this week at Hamstall in young Edward's removal to school. He is going to Rugby, and is very happy in the idea of it; I wish his happiness may last, but it will be a great change to become a raw school-boy from being a pompous sermon-writer and a domineering brother. It will do him good, I dare say.

Caroline has had a great escape from being burnt to death lately. As her husband gives the account, we must believe it true. Miss Murden is gone,—called away by the critical state of Mrs. Pottinger who has had another severe stroke, and is without sense or speech. Miss Murden wishes to return to Southampton if circumstances suit, but it must be very doubtful.

We have been obliged to turn away Cholles, he grew so very drunken and negligent, and we have a man in his place called Thomas.

Martha desires me to communicate something concerning herself which she knows will give you pleasure, as affording her very particular satisfaction,—it is that she is to be in town this spring with Mrs. Dundas. I need not dilate on the subject. You understand enough of the whys and wherefores to enter into her feelings, and to be conscious that of all possible arrangements it is the one most acceptable to her. She goes to Barton on leaving us, and the family remove to town in April.

What you tell me of Miss Sharpe is quite new, and surprises

me a little; I feel, however, as you do. She is born, poor thing! to struggle with evil, and her continuing with Miss B. is, I hope, a proof that matters are not always so very bad between them as her letters sometimes represent.

Jenny's marriage I had heard of, and supposed you would do so too from Steventon, as I knew you were corresponding with Mary at the time. I hope she will not sully the respectable name she now bears.

Your plan for Miss Curling is uncommonly considerate and friendly, and such as she must surely jump at. Edward's going round by Steventon, as I understand he promises to do, can be no reasonable objection; Mrs. J. Austen's hospitality is just of the kind to enjoy such a visitor.

We were very glad to know Aunt Fanny was in the country when we read of the fire. Pray give my best compliments to the Mrs. Finches, if they are at Gm. I am sorry to find that Sir J. Moore has a mother living, but though a very heroic son he might not be a very necessary one to her happiness. Deacon Morrell may be more to Mrs. Morrell.

I wish Sir John had united something of the Christian with the hero in his death. Thank heaven! we have had no one to care for particularly among the troops,—no one, in fact, nearer to us than Sir John himself. Col. Maitland is safe and well; his mother and sisters were of course anxious about him, but there is no entering much into the solicitudes of that family.

My mother is well, and gets out when she can with the same enjoyment, and apparently the same strength, as hitherto. She hopes you will not omit begging Mrs. Seward to get the garden cropped for us, supposing she leaves the house too early to make the garden any object to herself. We are very desirous of receiving your account of the house, for your observations will have a motive which can leave nothing to conjecture and suffer nothing from want of memory. For one's own dear self, one ascertains and remembers everything.

Lady Sondes is an impudent woman to come back into her

old neighborhood again; I suppose she pretends never to have married before, and wonders how her father and mother came to have her christened Lady Sondes.

The store-closet, I hope, will never do so again, for much of the evil is proved to have proceeded from the gutter being choked up, and we have had it cleared. We had reason to rejoice in the child's absence at the time of the thaw, for the nursery was not habitable. We hear of similar disasters from almost everybody.

No news from Portsmouth. We are very patient. Mrs. Charles Fowle desires to be kindly remembered to you. She is warmly interested in my brother and his family.

Yours very affectionately,
J. AUSTEN.

Miss AUSTEN, EDWARD AUSTEN'S, Esq.,
Godmersham Park, Faversham, Kent.

XXXV.

SLOANE ST., Thursday (April 18, 1811).

MY DEAR CASSANDRA,—I have so many little matters to tell you of, that I cannot wait any longer before I begin to put them down. I spent Tuesday in Bentinck Street. The Cookes called here and took me back, and it was quite a Cooke day, for the Miss Rolles paid a visit while I was there, and Sam Arnold dropped in to tea.

The badness of the weather disconcerted an excellent plan of mine,—that of calling on Miss Beckford again; but from the middle of the day it rained incessantly. Mary and I, after disposing of her father and mother, went to the Liverpool Museum and the British Gallery, and I had some amusement at each, though my preference for men and women always inclines me to attend more to the company than the sight.

Mrs. Cooke regrets very much that she did not see you when you called; it was owing to a blunder among the servants, for she did not know of our visit till we were gone. She seems tolerably well, but the nervous part of her complaint, I fear, increases, and makes her more and more unwilling to part with Mary.

I have proposed to the latter that she should go to Chawton with me, on the supposition of my travelling the Guildford road, and she, I do believe, would be glad to do it, but perhaps it may be impossible; unless a brother can be at home at that time, it certainly must. George comes to them to-day.

I did not see Theo. till late on Tuesday; he was gone to Ilford, but he came back in time to show his usual nothing-meaning, harmless, heartless civility. Henry, who had been confined the whole day to the bank, took me in his way home, and, after putting life and wit into the party for a quarter of an hour, put himself and his sister into a hackney coach.

I bless my stars that I have done with Tuesday. But, alas! Wednesday was likewise a day of great doings, for Manon and I took our walk to Grafton House, and I have a good deal to say on that subject.

I am sorry to tell you that I am getting very extravagant, and spending all my money, and, what is worse for you, I have been spending yours too; for in a linendraper's shop to which I went for checked muslin, and for which I was obliged to give seven shillings a yard, I was tempted by a pretty-colored muslin, and bought ten yards of it on the chance of your liking it; but at the same time, if it should not suit you, you must not think yourself at all obliged to take it; it is only 3s. 6d. per yard, and I should not in the least mind keeping the whole. In texture it is just what we prefer, but its resemblance to green crewels, I must own, is not great, for the pattern is a small red spot. And now I believe I have done all my commissions except Wedgwood.

I liked my walk very much; it was shorter than I had expected, and the weather was delightful. We set off immediately after breakfast, and must have reached Grafton House by half-past eleven; but when we entered the shop the whole counter was thronged, and we waited full half an hour before we could be attended to. When we were served, however, I was very well satisfied with my purchases,—my bugle trimming at 2s. 4d. and three pair silk stockings for a little less than 12s. a pair.

In my way back who should I meet but Mr. Moore, just come from Beckenham. I believe he would have passed me if I had not made him stop, but we were delighted to meet. I soon found, however, that he had nothing new to tell me, and then I let him go.

Miss Burton has made me a very pretty little bonnet, and now nothing can satisfy me but I must have a straw hat, of the riding-hat shape, like Mrs. Tilson's; and a young woman in this neighborhood is actually making me one. I am really very shocking, but it will not be dear at a guinea. Our pelisses are 17s. each; she charges only 8s. for the making, but the buttons seem expensive,—are expensive, I might have said, for the fact is plain enough.

We drank tea again yesterday with the Tilsons, and met the Smiths. I find all these little parties very pleasant. I like Mrs. S.; Miss Beaty is good-humor itself, and does not seem much besides. We spend to-morrow evening with them, and are to meet the Coln. and Mrs. Cantelo Smith you have been used to hear of, and, if she is in good humor, are likely to have excellent singing.

To-night I might have been at the play; Henry had kindly planned our going together to the Lyceum, but I have a cold which I should not like to make worse before Saturday, so I stay within all this day.

Eliza is walking out by herself. She has plenty of business on her hands just now, for the day of the party is settled, and drawing near. Above eighty people are invited for next Tuesday evening, and there is to be some very good music,—five professionals, three of them glee singers, besides amateurs. Fanny will listen to this. One of the hirelings is a Capital on the harp, from which I expect great pleasure. The foundation of the party was a dinner to Henry Egerton and Henry Walter, but the latter leaves town the day before. I am sorry, as I wished her prejudice to be done away, but should have been more sorry if there had been no invitation.

I am a wretch, to be so occupied with all these things as to seem to have no thoughts to give to people and circumstances which really supply a far more lasting interest,—the society in which you are; but I do think of you all, I assure you, and want to know all about everybody, and especially about your visit to the W. Friars; *mais le moyen* not to be occupied by one's own concerns?

Saturday.—Frank is superseded in the "Caledonia." Henry brought us this news yesterday from Mr. Daysh, and he heard at the same time that Charles may be in England in the course of a month. Sir Edward Pollen succeeds Lord Gambier in his command, and some captain of his succeeds Frank; and I believe the order is already gone out. Henry means to inquire further to-day. He wrote to Mary on the occasion. This is something to think of. Henry is convinced that he will have the offer of something else, but does not think it will be at all incumbent on him to accept it; and then follows, what will he do? and where will he live?

I hope to hear from you to-day. How are you as to health, strength, looks, etc.? I had a very comfortable account from Chawton yesterday.

If the weather permits, Eliza and I walk into London this morning. She is in want of chimney lights for Tuesday, and I of an ounce of darning-cotton. She has resolved not to venture to the play to-night. The D'Entraigues and Comte Julien cannot come to the party, which was at first a grief, but she has since supplied herself so well with performers that it is of no consequence; their not coming has produced our going to them to-morrow evening, which I like the idea of. It will be amusing to see the ways of a French circle.

I wrote to Mrs. Hill a few days ago, and have received a most kind and satisfactory answer. Any time the first week in May exactly suits her, and therefore I consider my going as tolerably fixed. I shall leave Sloane Street on the 1st or 2d, and be ready for James on the 9th, and, if his plan alters, I can take care of myself. I have explained my views here, and everything is smooth and pleasant; and Eliza talks kindly of conveying me to Streatham.

We met the Tilsons yesterday evening, but the singing Smiths sent an excuse, which put our Mrs. Smith out of humor.

We are come back, after a good dose of walking and coaching, and I have the pleasure of your letter. I wish I had James's verses, but they were left at Chawton. When I return thither, if Mrs. K. will give me leave, I will send them to her.

Our first object to-day was Henrietta St., to consult with Henry in consequence of a very unlucky change of the play for this very night,—"Hamlet" instead of "King John,"— and we are to go on Monday to "Macbeth" instead; but it is a

disappointment to us both.
Love to all.

Yours affectionately,
JANE.

Miss AUSTEN, EDWARD AUSTEN'S, Esq.,
Godmersham Park, Faversham, Kent.

XXXVI.

SLOANE ST., Thursday (April 25).

MY DEAREST CASSANDRA,—I can return the compliment by thanking you for the unexpected pleasure of your letter yesterday, and as I like unexpected pleasure, it made me very happy; and, indeed, you need not apologize for your letter in any respect, for it is all very fine, but not too fine, I hope, to be written again, or something like it.

I think Edward will not suffer much longer from heat; by the look of things this morning I suspect the weather is rising into the balsamic north-east. It has been hot here, as you may suppose, since it was so hot with you, but I have not suffered from it at all, nor felt it in such a degree as to make me imagine it would be anything in the country. Everybody has talked of the heat, but I set it all down to London.

I give you joy of our new nephew, and hope if he ever comes to be hanged it will not be till we are too old to care about it. It is a great comfort to have it so safely and speedily over. The Miss Curlings must be hard worked in writing so many letters, but the novelty of it may recommend it to them; mine was from Miss Eliza, and she says that my brother may arrive to-day.

No, indeed, I am never too busy to think of S. and S.[13] I can no more forget it than a mother can forget her sucking child; and I am much obliged to you for your inquiries. I have had two sheets to correct, but the last only brings us to Willoughby's first appearance. Mrs. K. regrets in the most flattering manner that she must wait till May, but I have scarcely a hope of its being out in June. Henry does not neglect it; he has hurried the printer, and says he will see him again to-day. It will not stand still during his absence, it will be sent to Eliza.

The Incomes remain as they were, but I will get them altered if I can. I am very much gratified by Mrs. K.'s interest in it; and whatever may be the event of it as to my credit with her, sincerely wish her curiosity could be satisfied sooner than is now probable. I think she will like my Elinor, but cannot build on anything else.

Our party went off extremely well. There were many solicitudes, alarms, and vexations beforehand, of course, but at last everything was quite right. The rooms were dressed up with flowers, etc., and looked very pretty. A glass for the mantelpiece was lent by the man who is making their own. Mr. Egerton and Mr. Walter came at half-past five, and the festivities began with a pair of very fine soles.

Yes, Mr. Walter—for he postponed his leaving London on purpose—which did not give much pleasure at the time, any more than the circumstance from which it rose,—his calling on Sunday and being asked by Henry to take the family dinner on that day, which he did; but it is all smoothed over now, and she likes him very well.

At half-past seven arrived the musicians in two hackney coaches, and by eight the lordly company began to appear. Among the earliest were George and Mary Cooke, and I spent the greatest part of the evening very pleasantly with them. The drawing-room being soon hotter than we liked, we placed ourselves in the connecting passage, which was comparatively cool, and gave us all the advantage of the music at a pleasant distance, as well as that of the first view of every new-comer.

I was quite surrounded by acquaintance, especially gentlemen; and what with Mr. Hampson, Mr. Seymour, Mr. W. Knatchbull, Mr. Guillemarde, Mr. Cure, a Captain Simpson, brother to *the* Captain Simpson, besides Mr. Walter and Mr. Egerton, in addition to the Cookes, and Miss Beckford, and Miss Middleton, I had quite as much upon my hands as I could do.

Poor Miss B. has been suffering again from her old complaint, and looks thinner than ever. She certainly goes to Cheltenham the beginning of June. We were all delight and cordiality, of course. Miss M. seems very happy, but has not beauty enough to figure in London.

Including everybody we were sixty-six,—which was considerably more than Eliza had expected, and quite enough to fill the back drawing-room and leave a few to be scattered about in the other and in the passage.

The music was extremely good. It opened (tell Fanny) with "Poike de Parp pirs praise pof Prapela;" and of the other glees I remember, "In peace love tunes," "Rosabelle," "The Red Cross Knight," and "Poor Insect." Between the songs were lessons on the harp, or harp and pianoforte together; and the harp-player was Wiepart, whose name seems famous, though new to me. There was one female singer, a short Miss Davis, all in blue, bringing up for the public line, whose voice was said to be very fine indeed; and all the performers gave great satisfaction by doing what they were paid for, and giving themselves no airs. No amateur could be persuaded to do anything.

The house was not clear till after twelve. If you wish to hear more of it, you must put your questions, but I seem rather to have exhausted than spared the subject.

This said Captain Simpson told us, on the authority of some other Captain just arrived from Halifax, that Charles was bringing the "Cleopatra" home, and that she was probably by this time in the Channel; but as Captain S. was certainly in liquor, we must not quite depend on it. It must give one a sort of expectation, however, and will prevent my writing to him any more. I would rather he should not reach England till I am at home, and the Steventon party gone.

My mother and Martha both write with great satisfaction of Anna's behavior. She is quite an Anna with variations, but she cannot have reached her last, for that is always the most flourishing and showy; she is at about her third or fourth, which are generally simple and pretty.

Your lilacs are in leaf, ours are in bloom. The horse-chestnuts are quite out, and the elms almost. I had a pleasant walk in Kensington Gardens on Sunday with Henry, Mr. Smith, and Mr. Tilson; everything was fresh and beautiful.

We did go to the play, after all, on Saturday. We went to the Lyceum, and saw the "Hypocrite," an old play taken from Molière's "Tartuffe," and were well entertained. Dowton and Mathews were the good actors; Mrs. Edwin was the heroine, and her performance is just what it used to be. I have no chance of seeing Mrs. Siddons; she did act on Monday, but as Henry was told by the box-keeper that he did not think she would, the plans, and all thought of it, were given up. I should particularly have liked seeing her in "Constance," and could swear at her with little effort for disappointing me.

Henry has been to the Water-Color Exhibition, which opened on Monday, and is to meet us there again some morning. If Eliza cannot go (and she has a cold at present), Miss Beaty will be invited to be my companion. Henry leaves town on Sunday afternoon, but he means to write soon himself to Edward, and will tell his own plans.

The tea is this moment setting out.

Do not have your colored muslin unless you really want it, because I am afraid I could not send it to the coach without giving trouble here.

Eliza caught her cold on Sunday in our way to the D'Entraigues. The horses actually gibbed on this side of Hyde Park Gate: a load of fresh gravel made it a formidable hill to them, and they refused the collar; I believe there was a sore shoulder to irritate. Eliza was frightened, and we got out, and were detained in the evening air several minutes. The cold is in her chest, but she takes care of herself, and I hope it may not last long.

This engagement prevented Mr. Walter's staying late,—he had his coffee and went away. Eliza enjoyed her evening very much, and means to cultivate the acquaintance; and I see nothing to dislike in them but their taking quantities of snuff. Monsieur, the old Count, is a very fine-looking man, with quiet manners, good enough for an Englishman, and, I believe, is a man of great information and taste. He has some fine paintings, which delighted Henry as much as the son's music gratified Eliza; and among them a miniature of Philip V. of Spain, Louis XIV.'s grandson, which exactly suited my capacity. Count Julien's performance is very wonderful.

We met only Mrs. Latouche and Miss East, and we are just now engaged to spend next Sunday evening at Mrs. L.'s, and to meet the D'Entraigues, but M. le Comte must do without Henry. If he would but speak English, I would take to him.

Have you ever mentioned the leaving off tea to Mrs. K.? Eliza has just spoken of it again. The benefit she has found from it in sleeping has been very great.

I shall write soon to Catherine to fix my day, which will be Thursday. We have no engagement but for Sunday. Eliza's cold makes quiet advisable. Her party is mentioned in this morning's paper. I am sorry to hear of poor Fanny's state. From that quarter, I suppose, is to be the alloy of her happiness. I will have no more to say.

Yours affectionately,
J. A.

Give my love particularly to my goddaughter.

Miss AUSTEN, EDWARD AUSTEN's, Esq.,
Godmersham Park, Faversham.

FOOTNOTES:

[13] "Sense and Sensibility."

XXXVII.

SLOANE ST., Tuesday.

MY DEAR CASSANDRA,—I had sent off my letter yesterday before yours came, which I was sorry for; but as Eliza has been so good as to get me a frank, your questions shall be answered without much further expense to you.

The best direction to Henry at Oxford will be "The Blue Boar, Cornmarket."

I do not mean to provide another trimming for my pelisse, for I am determined to spend no more money; so I shall wear it as it is, longer than I ought, and then—I do not know.

My head-dress was a bugle-band like the border to my gown, and a flower of Mrs. Tilson's. I depended upon hearing something of the evening from Mr. W. K., and am very well satisfied with his notice of me—"A pleasing-looking young woman"—that must do; one cannot pretend to anything better now; thankful to have it continued a few years longer!

It gives me sincere pleasure to hear of Mrs. Knight's having had a tolerable night at last, but upon this occasion I wish she had another name, for the two *nights* jingle very much.

We have tried to get "Self-control," but in vain. I should like to know what her estimate is, but am always half afraid of finding a clever novel too clever, and of finding my own story and my own people all forestalled.

Eliza has just received a few lines from Henry to assure her of the good conduct of his mare. He slept at Uxbridge on Sunday, and wrote from Wheatfield.

We were not claimed by Hans Place yesterday, but are to dine there to-day. Mr. Tilson called in the evening, but otherwise we were quite alone all day; and after having been out a good deal, the change was very pleasant.

I like your opinion of Miss Atten much better than I expected, and have now hopes of her staying a whole twelvemonth. By this time I suppose she is hard at it, governing away. Poor creature! I pity her, though they are my nieces.

Oh! yes, I remember Miss Emma Plumbtree's local consequence perfectly.

> I am in a dilemma, for want of an Emma,
> Escaped from the lips of Henry Gipps.

But, really, I was never much more put to it than in continuing an answer to Fanny's former message. What is there to be said on the subject? Pery pell, or pare pey? or po; or at the most, Pi, pope, pey, pike, pit.

I congratulate Edward on the Weald of Kent Canal Bill being put off till another Session, as I have just had the pleasure of reading. There is always something to be hoped from delay.

> Between Session and Session
> The first Prepossession
> May rouse up the Nation,
> And the villanous Bill
> May be forced to lie still
> Against wicked men's will.

There is poetry for Edward and his daughter. I am afraid I shall not have any for you.

I forgot to tell you in my last that our cousin Miss Payne called in on Saturday, and was persuaded to stay dinner. She told us a great deal about her friend Lady Cath. Brecknell, who is most happily married, and Mr. Brecknell is very religious, and has got black whiskers.

I am glad to think that Edward has a tolerable day for his drive to Goodnestone, and very glad to hear of his kind promise of bringing you to town. I hope everything will arrange itself favorably. The 16th is now to be Mrs. Dundas's day.

I mean, if I can, to wait for your return before I have my new gown made up, from a notion of their making up to more advantage together; and as I find the muslin is not so wide as it used to be, some contrivance may be necessary. I expect the skirt to require one-half breadth cut in gores, besides two whole breadths.

Eliza has not yet quite resolved on inviting Anna, but I think she will.

Yours very affectionately,
JANE.

XXXVIII.

CHAWTON, Wednesday (May 29).

IT was a mistake of mine, my dear Cassandra, to talk of a tenth child at Hamstall. I had forgot there were but eight already.

Your inquiry after my uncle and aunt were most happily timed, for the very same post brought an account of them. They are again at Gloucester House enjoying fresh air, which they seem to have felt the want of in Bath, and are tolerably well, but not more than tolerable. My aunt does not enter into particulars, but she does not write in spirits, and we imagine that she has never entirely got the better of her disorder in the winter. Mrs. Welby takes her out airing in her barouche, which gives her a headache,—a comfortable proof, I suppose, of the uselessness of the new carriage when they have got it.

You certainly must have heard before I can tell you that Col. Orde has married our cousin Margt. Beckford, the Marchess. of Douglas's sister. The papers say that her father disinherits her, but I think too well of an Orde to suppose that she has not a handsome independence of her own.

Chawton Cottage, from the Garden
LETTERS, 172

The chickens are all alive and fit for the table, but we save them for something grand. Some of the flower seeds are coming up very well, but your mignonette makes a wretched appearance. Miss Benn has been equally unlucky as to hers. She had seed from four different people, and none of it comes up. Our young piony at the foot of the fir-tree has just blown and looks very handsome, and the whole of the shrubbery border will soon be very gay with pinks and sweet-williams, in addition to the columbines already in bloom. The syringas, too, are coming out. We are likely to have a great crop of Orleans plums, but not many greengages—on the standard scarcely any, three or four dozen, perhaps, against the wall. I believe I told you differently when I first came home, but I can now judge better than I could then.

I have had a medley and satisfactory letter this morning from the husband and wife at Cowes; and in consequence of what is related of their plans, we have been talking over the possibility of inviting them here in their way from Steventon, which is what one should wish to do, and is, I dare say, what they expect, but, supposing Martha to be at home, it does not seem a very easy

147

thing to accommodate so large a party. My mother offers to give up her room to Frank and Mary, but there will then be only the best for two maids and three children.

They go to Steventon about the 22d, and I guess—for it is quite a guess—will stay there from a fortnight to three weeks.

I must not venture to press Miss Sharpe's coming at present; we may hardly be at liberty before August.

Poor John Bridges! we are very sorry for his situation and for the distress of the family. Lady B., is in one way severely tried. And our own dear brother suffers a great deal, I dare say, on the occasion.

I have not much to say of ourselves. Anna is nursing a cold caught in the arbor at Faringdon, that she may be able to keep her engagement to Maria M. this evening, when I suppose she will make it worse.

She did not return from Faringdon till Sunday, when H. B. walked home with her, and drank tea here. She was with the Prowtings almost all Monday. She went to learn to make feather trimmings of Miss Anna, and they kept her to dinner, which was rather lucky, as we were called upon to meet Mrs. and Miss Terry the same evening at the Digweeds; and though Anna was of course invited too, I think it always safest to keep her away from the family, lest she should be doing too little or too much.

Mrs. Terry, Mary, and Robert, with my aunt Harding and her daughter, came from Dummer for a day and a night,—all very agreeable and very much delighted with the new house and with Chawton in general.

We sat upstairs, and had thunder and lightning as usual. I never knew such a spring for thunderstorms as it has been. Thank God! we have had no bad ones here. I thought myself in luck to have my uncomfortable feelings shared by the mistress of the house, as that procured blinds and candles. It had been excessively hot the whole day. Mrs. Harding is a good-looking woman, but not much like Mrs. Toke, inasmuch as she is very brown and has scarcely any teeth; she seems to have some of Mrs.

Toke's civility. Miss H. is an elegant, pleasing, pretty-looking girl, about nineteen, I suppose, or nineteen and a half, or nineteen and a quarter, with flowers in her head and music at her finger-ends. She plays very well indeed. I have seldom heard anybody with more pleasure. They were at Godington four or five years ago. My cousin Flora Long was there last year.

My name is Diana. How does Fanny like it? What a change in the weather! We have a fire again now.

Harriet Benn sleeps at the Great House to-night, and spends to-morrow with us; and the plan is that we should all walk with her to drink tea at Faringdon, for her mother is now recovered; but the state of the weather is not very promising at present.

Miss Benn has been returned to her cottage since the beginning of last week, and has now just got another girl; she comes from Alton. For many days Miss B. had nobody with her but her niece Elizabeth, who was delighted to be her visitor and her maid. They both dined here on Saturday while Anna was at Faringdon; and last night an accidental meeting and a sudden impulse produced Miss Benn and Maria Middleton at our tea-table.

If you have not heard it is very fit you should, that Mr. Harrison has had the living of Fareham given him by the Bishop, and is going to reside there; and now it is said that Mr. Peach (beautiful wiseacre) wants to have the curacy of Overton, and if he does leave Wootton, James Digweed wishes to go there. Fare you well.

Yours affectionately,
JANE AUSTEN.

The chimneys at the Great House are done. Mr. Prowting has opened a gravel-pit, very conveniently for my mother, just at the mouth of the approach to his house; but it looks a little as if he meant to catch all his company. Tolerable gravel.

Miss AUSTEN,
Godmersham Park, Faversham, Kent.

XXXIX.

CHAWTON, Thursday (June 6).

By this time, my dearest Cassandra, you know Martha's plans. I was rather disappointed, I confess, to find that she could not leave town till after ye 24th, as I had hoped to see you here the week before. The delay, however, is not great, and everything seems generally arranging itself for your return very comfortably.

I found Henry perfectly predisposed to bring you to London if agreeable to yourself; he has not fixed his day for going into Kent, but he must be back again before ye 20th. You may therefore think with something like certainty of the close of your Godmersham visit, and will have, I suppose, about a week for Sloane Street. He travels in his gig, and should the weather be tolerable I think you must have a delightful journey.

I have given up all idea of Miss Sharpe's travelling with you and Martha, for though you are both all compliance with my scheme, yet as you knock off a week from the end of her visit, and Martha rather more from the beginning, the thing is out of the question.

I have written to her to say that after the middle of July we shall be happy to receive her, and I have added a welcome if she could make her way hither directly, but I do not expect that she will. I have also sent our invitation to Cowes.

We are very sorry for the disappointment you have all had in Lady B.'s illness; but a division of the proposed party is with you by this time, and I hope may have brought you a better account of the rest.

Give my love and thanks to Harriot, who has written me charming things of your looks, and diverted me very much by poor Mrs. C. Milles's continued perplexity.

I had a few lines from Henry on Tuesday to prepare us for himself and his friend, and by the time that I had made the sumptuous provision of a neck of mutton on the occasion, they drove into the court; but lest you should not immediately recollect in how many hours a neck of mutton may be certainly procured, I add that they came a little after twelve,—both tall and well, and in their different degrees agreeable.

It was a visit of only twenty-four hours, but very pleasant while it lasted. Mr. Tilson took a sketch of the Great House before dinner, and after dinner we all three walked to Chawton Park,[14] meaning to go into it, but it was too dirty, and we were obliged to keep on the outside. Mr. Tilson admired the trees very much, but grieved that they should not be turned into money.

My mother's cold is better, and I believe she only wants dry weather to be very well. It was a great distress to her that Anna should be absent during her uncle's visit, a distress which I could not share. She does not return from Faringdon till this evening, and I doubt not has had plenty of the miscellaneous, unsettled sort of happiness which seems to suit her best. We hear from Miss Benn, who was on the Common with the Prowtings, that she was very much admired by the gentlemen in general.

I like your new bonnets exceedingly; yours is a shape which always looks well, and I think Fanny's particularly becoming to her.

On Monday I had the pleasure of receiving, unpacking, and approving our Wedgwood ware. It all came very safely, and upon the whole is a good match, though I think they might have allowed us rather larger leaves, especially in such a year of fine foliage as this. One is apt to suppose that the woods about Birmingham must be blighted. There was no bill with the goods, but that shall not screen them from being paid. I mean to ask Martha to settle the account. It will be quite in her way, for she is just now sending my mother a breakfast-set from the same place.

I hope it will come by the wagon to-morrow; it is certainly what we want, and I long to know what it is like, and as I am sure Martha has great pleasure in making the present, I will not have any regret. We have considerable dealings with the wagons at present: a hamper of port and brandy from Southampton is now in the kitchen.

Your answer about the Miss Plumbtrees proves you as fine a Daniel as ever Portia was; for I maintained Emma to be the eldest.

We began pease on Sunday, but our gatherings are very small, not at all like the gathering in the "Lady of the Lake." Yesterday I had the agreeable surprise of finding several scarlet strawberries quite ripe; had you been at home, this would have been a pleasure lost. There are more gooseberries and fewer currants than I thought at first. We must buy currants for our wine.

The Digweeds are gone down to see the Stephen Terrys at Southampton, and catch the King's birthday at Portsmouth. Miss Papillon called on us yesterday, looking handsomer than ever. Maria Middleton and Miss Benn dine here to-morrow.

We are not to enclose any more letters to Abingdon Street, as perhaps Martha has told you.

I had just left off writing and put on my things for walking to Alton, when Anna and her friend Harriot called in their way thither; so we went together. Their business was to provide mourning against the King's death, and my mother has had a bombazine bought for her. I am not sorry to be back again, for the young ladies had a great deal to do, and without much method in doing it.

Anna does not come home till to-morrow morning. She has written I find to Fanny, but there does not seem to be a great deal to relate of Tuesday. I had hoped there might be dancing.

Mrs. Budd died on Sunday evening. I saw her two days before her death, and thought it must happen soon. She suffered much from weakness and restlessness almost to the last. Poor little Harriot seems truly grieved. You have never mentioned

Harry; how is he?
    With love to you all,

                                        Yours affectionately,
                                                J. A.

Miss AUSTEN, EDWARD AUSTEN'S, Esq.,
Godmersham Park, Faversham.

FOOTNOTE:

[14] A large beech wood extending for a long distance upon a hill
about a mile from Chawton: the trees are magnificent.

XL.

CHAWTON, Friday (January 29, 1813).

I HOPE you received my little parcel by J. Bond on Wednesday evening, my dear Cassandra, and that you will be ready to hear from me again on Sunday, for I feel that I must write to you to-day. I want to tell you that I have got my own darling child[15] from London. On Wednesday I received one copy sent down by Falkener, with three lines from Henry to say that he had given another to Charles and sent a third by the coach to Godmersham.... The advertisement is in our paper to-day for the first time: 18s. He shall ask 1l. 1s. for my two next, and 1l. 8s. for my stupidest of all. Miss B. dined with us on the very day of the book's coming, and in the evening we fairly set at it, and read half the first vol. to her, prefacing that, having intelligence from Henry that such a work would soon appear, we had desired him to send it whenever it came out, and I believe it passed with her unsuspected. She was amused, poor soul! *That* she could not help, you know, with two such people to lead the way; but she really does seem to admire Elizabeth. I must confess that I think her as delightful a creature as ever appeared in print, and how I shall be able to tolerate those who do not like *her* at least, I do not know. There are a few typical errors; and a "said he," or a "said she," would sometimes make the dialogue more immediately clear; but "I do not write for such dull elves" as have not a great deal of ingenuity themselves. The second volume is shorter than I could wish, but the difference is not so much in reality as in look, there being a larger proportion of narrative in that part. I have lop't and crop't so successfully, however, that I imagine it must be rather shorter than "Sense and Sensibility" altogether. Now I will try and write of something else.

FOOTNOTES:

[15] "Pride and Prejudice."

XLI.

CHAWTON, Thursday (February 4).

MY DEAR CASSANDRA,—Your letter was truly welcome, and I am much obliged to you for all your praise; it came at a right time, for I had had some fits of disgust. Our second evening's reading to Miss B. had not pleased me so well, but I believe something must be attributed to my mother's too rapid way of getting on: though she perfectly understands the characters herself, she cannot speak as they ought. Upon the whole, however, I am quite vain enough and well satisfied enough. The work is rather too light and bright and sparkling: it wants shade; it wants to be stretched out here and there with a long chapter of sense, if it could be had; if not, of solemn specious nonsense, about something unconnected with the story,—an essay on writing, a critique on Walter Scott, or the history of Buonaparte, or something that would form a contrast, and bring the reader with increased delight to the playfulness and epigrammatism of the general style.... The greatest blunder in the printing that I have met with is in page 220, v. 3, where two speeches are made into one. There might as well be no suppers at Longbourn; but I suppose it was the remains of Mrs. Bennet's old Meryton habits.

XLII.

THIS will be a quick return for yours, my dear Cassandra. I doubt its having much else to recommend it; but there is no saying: it may turn out to be a very long and delightful letter. I am exceedingly pleased that you can say what you do, after having gone through the whole work, and Fanny's praise is very gratifying. My hopes were tolerably strong of her, but nothing like a certainty. Her liking Darcy and Elizabeth is enough. She might hate all the others, if she would. I have her opinion under her own hand this morning; but your transcript of it, which I read first, was not, and is not, the less acceptable. To me it is of course all praise, but the more exact truth which she sends you is good enough.... Our party on Wednesday was not unagreeable, though we wanted a master of the house less anxious and fidgety, and more conversable. Upon Mrs. ——'s mentioning that she had sent the rejected addresses to Mrs. H., I began talking to her a little about them, and expressed my hope of their having amused her. Her answer was, "Oh dear, yes, very much, very droll indeed, the opening of the house, and the striking up of the fiddles!" What she meant, poor woman, who shall say? I sought no farther. As soon as a whist-party was formed, and a round table threatened, I made my mother an excuse and came away, leaving just as many for their round table as there were at Mrs. Grant's.[16] I wish they might be as agreeable a set. My mother is very well, and finds great amusement in glove-knitting, and at present wants no other work. We quite run over with books. She has got Sir John Carr's "Travels in Spain," and I am reading a

Society octavo, an "Essay on the Military Police and Institutions of the British Empire," by Capt. Pasley of the Engineers,—a book which I protested against at first, but which upon trial I find delightfully written and highly entertaining. I am as much in love with the author as I ever was with Clarkson or Buchanan, or even the two Mr. Smiths of the city. The first soldier I ever sighed for; but he does write with extraordinary force and spirit. Yesterday, moreover, brought us "Mrs. Grant's Letters," with Mr. White's compliments; but I have disposed of them, compliments and all, to Miss P., and amongst so many readers or retainers of books as we have in Chawton, I dare say there will be no difficulty in getting rid of them for another fortnight, if necessary. I have disposed of Mrs. Grant for the second fortnight to Mrs. ——. It can make no difference to her which of the twenty-six fortnights in the year the three vols. lie on her table. I have been applied to for information as to the oath taken in former times of Bell, Book, and Candle, but have none to give. Perhaps you may be able to learn something of its origin where you now are. Ladies who read those enormous great stupid thick quarto volumes which one always sees in the breakfast-parlor there must be acquainted with everything in the world. I detest a quarto. Captain Pasley's book is too good for their society. They will not understand a man who condenses his thoughts into an octavo. I have learned from Sir J. Carr that there is no Government House at Gibraltar. I must alter it to the Commissioner's.

FOOTNOTES:

[16] At this time, February, 1813, "Mansfield Park" was nearly finished.

XLIII.

SLOANE STREET, Thursday, May 20.

MY DEAR CASSANDRA,—Before I say anything else, I claim a paper full of halfpence on the drawing-room mantelpiece; I put them there myself, and forgot to bring them with me. I cannot say that I have yet been in any distress for money, but I choose to have my due, as well as the Devil. How lucky we were in our weather yesterday! This wet morning makes one more sensible of it. We had no rain of any consequence. The head of the curricle was put half up three or four times, but our share of the showers was very trifling, though they seemed to be heavy all round us, when we were on the Hog's-back, and I fancied it might then be raining so hard at Chawton as to make you feel for us much more than we deserved. Three hours and a quarter took us to Guildford, where we stayed barely two hours, and had only just time enough for all we had to do there; that is, eating a long and comfortable breakfast, watching the carriages, paying Mr. Harrington, and taking a little stroll afterwards. From some views which that stroll gave us, I think most highly of the situation of Guildford. We wanted all our brothers and sisters to be standing with us in the bowling-green, and looking towards Horsham. I was very lucky in my gloves,—got them at the first shop I went to, though I went into it rather because it was near than because it looked at all like a glove-shop, and gave only four shillings for them; after which everybody at Chawton will be hoping and predicting that they cannot be good for anything, and their worth certainly remains to be proved; but I think they look very well. We left Guildford at twenty minutes before twelve (I hope somebody cares for these minutiæ), and were at Esher in about two hours more. I was very much pleased with the country in general. Between Guildford and Ripley I thought it particularly pretty, also about Painshill; and from a Mr. Spicer's grounds at Esher, which we walked into before dinner, the views were beautiful. I cannot say what we did *not* see, but I should think there could not be a wood, or a meadow, or palace, or remarkable spot in England that was not spread out before us on one side or other. Claremont is going to be sold: a Mr. Ellis has it now. It is a house that seems never to have prospered. After dinner we walked forward to be overtaken at the coachman's time, and before he did overtake us we were very near Kingston. I fancy it was about half-past six when we reached this house,—a twelve hours' business, and the horses did not appear more than reasonably tired. I was very tired too, and glad to get to bed early, but am quite well to-day. I am very snug in the front drawing-room all to myself, and would not say "thank you" for any company but you. The quietness of it does me good. I have contrived to pay my two visits, though the weather made me a great while about it, and left me only a few minutes to sit with Charlotte Craven.[17] She looks very well, and her hair is done up with an elegance to do credit to any education. Her manners are as unaffected and pleasing as ever. She had heard from her mother to-day. Mrs. Craven spends another fortnight at Chilton. I saw nobody but Charlotte, which pleased me best. I was shown upstairs into a drawing-room, where she came to me; and the appearance of the room, so totally unschoollike, amused me very much: it was full of modern elegances.

Yours very affectly,
J. A.

FOOTNOTE:

[17] The present Lady Pollen, of Redenham, near Andover, then at a school in London.

XLIV.

SLOANE STREET, Monday (May 24).

MY DEAREST CASSANDRA,—I am very much obliged to you for writing to me. You must have hated it after a worrying morning. Your letter came just in time to save my going to Remnant's, and fit me for Christian's, where I bought Fanny's dimity.

I went the day before (Friday) to Layton's as I proposed, and got my mother's gown,—seven yards at 6s. 6d. I then walked into No. 10, which is all dirt and confusion, but in a very promising way; and after being present at the opening of a new account, to my great amusement, Henry and I went to the exhibition in Spring Gardens. It is not thought a good collection, but I was very well pleased, particularly (pray tell Fanny) with a small portrait of Mrs. Bingley,[18] excessively like her.

I went in hopes of seeing one of her sister, but there was no Mrs. Darcy.[18] Perhaps, however, I may find her in the great exhibition, which we shall go to if we have time. I have no chance of her in the collection of Sir Joshua Reynolds's paintings, which is now showing in Pall Mall, and which we are also to visit.

Mrs. Bingley's is exactly herself,—size, shaped face, features, and sweetness; there never was a greater likeness. She is dressed in a white gown, with green ornaments, which convinces me of what I had always supposed, that green was a favorite color with her. I dare say Mrs. D. will be in yellow.

Friday was our worst day as to weather. We were out in a very long and very heavy storm of hail, and there had been others before, but I heard no thunder. Saturday was a good deal better; dry and cold.

I gave 2*s*. 6*d*. for the dimity. I do not boast of any bargains, but think both the sarsenet and dimity good of their sort.

I have bought your locket, but was obliged to give 18*s*. for it, which must be rather more than you intended. It is neat and plain, set in gold.

We were to have gone to the Somerset House Exhibition on Saturday, but when I reached Henrietta Street Mr. Hampson was wanted there, and Mr. Tilson and I were obliged to drive about town after him, and by the time we had done it was too late for anything but home. We never found him after all.

I have been interrupted by Mrs. Tilson. Poor woman! She is in danger of not being able to attend Lady Drummond Smith's party to-night. Miss Burdett was to have taken her, and now Miss Burdett has a cough and will not go. My cousin Caroline is her sole dependence.

The events of yesterday were, our going to Belgrave Chapel in the morning, our being prevented by the rain from going to evening service at St. James, Mr. Hampson's calling, Messrs. Barlow and Phillips dining here, and Mr. and Mrs. Tilson's coming in the evening *à l'ordinaire*. She drank tea with us both Thursday and Saturday; he dined out each day, and on Friday we were with them, and they wish us to go to them to-morrow evening, to meet Miss Burdett, but I do not know how it will end. Henry talks of a drive to Hampstead, which may interfere with it.

I should like to see Miss Burdett very well, but that I am rather frightened by hearing that she wishes to be introduced to me. If I am a wild beast, I cannot help it. It is not my own fault.

There is no change in our plan of leaving London, but we shall not be with you before Tuesday. Henry thinks Monday would appear too early a day. There is no danger of our being induced to stay longer.

I have not quite determined how I shall manage about my clothes; perhaps there may be only my trunk to send by the coach, or there may be a band-box with it. I have taken your gentle hint, and written to Mrs. Hill.

The Hoblyns want us to dine with them, but we have refused. When Henry returns he will be dining out a great deal, I dare say; as he will then be alone, it will be more desirable; he will be more welcome at every table, and every invitation more welcome to him. He will not want either of us again till he is settled in Henrietta Street. This is my present persuasion. And he will not be settled there—really settled—till late in the autumn; "he will not be come to bide" till after September.

There is a gentleman in treaty for this house. Gentleman himself is in the country, but gentleman's friend came to see it the other day, and seemed pleased on the whole. Gentleman would rather prefer an increased rent to parting with five hundred guineas at once, and if that is the only difficulty it will not be minded. Henry is indifferent as to the which.

Get us the best weather you can for Wednesday, Thursday, and Friday. We are to go to Windsor in our way to Henley, which will be a great delight. We shall be leaving Sloane Street about twelve, two or three hours after Charles's party have begun their journey. You will miss them, but the comfort of getting back into your own room will be great. And then the tea and sugar!

I fear Miss Clewes is not better, or you would have mentioned it. I shall not write again unless I have any unexpected communication or opportunity to tempt me. I enclose Mr. Herington's bill and receipt.

I am very much obliged to Fanny for her letter; it made me laugh heartily, but I cannot pretend to answer it. Even had I more time, I should not feel at all sure of the sort of letter that Miss D.[19] would write. I hope Miss Benn is got well again, and will have a comfortable dinner with you to-day.

Monday Evening.—We have been both to the exhibition and Sir J. Reynolds's, and I am disappointed, for there was nothing like Mrs. D. at either. I can only imagine that Mr. D. prizes any picture of her too much to like it should be exposed to the public eye. I can imagine he would have that sort of feeling,—that mixture of love, pride, and delicacy.

Setting aside this disappointment, I had great amusement among the pictures; and the driving about, the carriage being open, was very pleasant. I liked my solitary elegance very much, and was ready to laugh all the time at my being where I was. I could not but feel that I had naturally small right to be parading about London in a barouche.

Henry desires Edward may know that he has just bought three dozen of claret for him (cheap), and ordered it to be sent down to Chawton.

I should not wonder if we got no farther than Reading on Thursday evening, and so reach Steventon only to a reasonable dinner-hour the next day; but whatever I may write or you may imagine, we know it will be something different. I shall be quiet to-morrow morning; all my business is done, and I shall only call again upon Mrs. Hoblyn, etc.

Love to your much ... party.

Yours affectionately,
J. AUSTEN.

FOOTNOTES:

[18] *Vide* "Pride and Prejudice."
[19] Miss Darcy.

XLV.

HENRIETTA ST., Wednesday (Sept. 15, ½ past 8).

HERE I am, my dearest Cassandra, seated in the breakfast, dining, sitting room, beginning with all my might. Fanny will join me as soon as she is dressed, and begin her letter.

We had a very good journey, weather and roads excellent; the three first stages for 1s. 6d., and our only misadventure the being delayed about a quarter of an hour at Kingston for horses, and being obliged to put up with a pair belonging to a hackney coach and their coachman, which left no room on the barouche box for Lizzy, who was to have gone her last stage there as she did the first; consequently we were all four within, which was a little crowded.

We arrived at a quarter-past four, and were kindly welcomed by the coachman, and then by his master, and then by William, and then by Mrs. Pengird, who all met us before we reached the foot of the stairs. Mde. Bigion was below dressing us a most comfortable dinner of soup, fish, bouillée, partridges, and an apple tart, which we sat down to soon after five, after cleaning and dressing ourselves, and feeling that we were most commodiously disposed of. The little adjoining dressing-room to our apartment makes Fanny and myself very well off indeed, and as we have poor Eliza's[20] bed our space is ample every way.

Sace arrived safely about half-past six. At seven we set off in a coach for the Lyceum; were at home again in about four hours and a half; had soup and wine and water, and then went to our holes.

Edward finds his quarters very snug and quiet. I must get a

softer pen. This is harder. I am in agonies. I have not yet seen Mr. Crabbe. Martha's letter is gone to the post.

I am going to write nothing but short sentences. There shall be two full stops in every line. Layton and Shear's is Bedford House. We mean to get there before breakfast if it's possible; for we feel more and more how much we have to do and how little time. This house looks very nice. It seems like Sloane Street moved here. I believe Henry is just rid of Sloane Street. Fanny does not come, but I have Edward seated by me beginning a letter, which looks natural.

Henry has been suffering from the pain in the face which he has been subject to before. He caught cold at Matlock, and since his return has been paying a little for past pleasure. It is nearly removed now, but he looks thin in the face, either from the pain or the fatigues of his tour, which must have been great.

Lady Robert is delighted with P. and P.,[21] and really was so, as I understand, before she knew who wrote it, for of course she knows now. He told her with as much satisfaction as if it were my wish. He did not tell me this, but he told Fanny. And Mr. Hastings! I am quite delighted with what such a man writes about it. Henry sent him the books after his return from Daylesford, but you will hear the letter too.

Let me be rational, and return to my two full stops.

I talked to Henry at the play last night. We were in a private box,—Mr. Spencer's,—which made it much more pleasant. The box is directly on the stage. One is infinitely less fatigued than in the common way. But Henry's plans are not what one could wish. He does not mean to be at Chawton till the 29th. He must be in town again by Oct. 5. His plan is to get a couple of days of pheasant shooting and then return directly. His wish was to bring you back with him. I have told him your scruples. He wishes you to suit yourself as to time, and if you cannot come till later, will send for you at any time as far as Bagshot. He presumed you would not find difficulty in getting so far. I could not say you would. He proposed your going with him into Oxfordshire. It was his own thought at first. I could not but catch at it for you.

We have talked of it again this morning (for now we have breakfasted), and I am convinced that if you can make it suit in other respects you need not scruple on his account. If you cannot come back with him on the 3rd or 4th, therefore, I do hope you will contrive to go to Adlestrop. By not beginning your absence till about the middle of this month I think you may manage it very well. But you will think all this over. One could wish he had intended to come to you earlier, but it cannot be helped.

I said nothing to him of Mrs. H. and Miss B., that he might not suppose difficulties. Shall not you put them into our own room? This seems to me the best plan, and the maid will be most conveniently near.

Oh, dear me! when I shall ever have done. We did go to Layton and Shear's before breakfast. Very pretty English poplins at 4s. 3d.; Irish, ditto at 6s.; more pretty, certainly,—beautiful.

Fanny and the two little girls are gone to take places for to-night at Covent Garden; "Clandestine Marriage" and "Midas." The latter will be a fine show for L. and M.[22] They revelled last night in "Don Juan," whom we left in hell at half-past eleven. We had scaramouch and a ghost, and were delighted. I speak of them; my delight was very tranquil, and the rest of us were sober-minded. "Don Juan" was the last of three musical things. "Five Hours at Brighton," in three acts,—of which one was over before we arrived, none the worse,—and the "Beehive," rather less flat and trumpery.

I have this moment received 5l. from kind, beautiful Edward. Fanny has a similar gift. I shall save what I can of it for your better leisure in this place. My letter was from Miss Sharpe,—nothing particular. A letter from Fanny Cage this morning.

Four o'clock.—We are just come back from doing Mrs. Tickars, Miss Hare, and Mr. Spence. Mr. Hall is here, and while Fanny is under his hands, I will try to write a little more.

Miss Hare had some pretty caps, and is to make me one like one of them, only white satin instead of blue. It will be white satin and lace, and a little white flower perking out of the left ear, like Harriot Byron's feather. I have allowed her to go as far as 1*l.* 16*s.* My gown is to be trimmed everywhere with white ribbon plaited on somehow or other. She says it will look well. I am not sanguine. They trim with white very much.

I learnt from Mrs. Tickars's young lady, to my high amusement, that the stays now are not made to force the bosom up at all; that was a very unbecoming, unnatural fashion. I was really glad to hear that they are not to be so much off the shoulders as they were.

Going to Mr. Spence's was a sad business, and cost us many tears; unluckily we were obliged to go a second time before he could do more than just look. We went first at half-past twelve and afterwards at three; papa with us each time; and, alas! we are to go again to-morrow. Lizzy is not finished yet. There have been no teeth taken out, however, nor will be, I believe; but he finds hers in a very bad state, and seems to think particularly ill of their durableness. They have been all cleaned, hers filed, and are to be filed again. There is a very sad hole between two of her front teeth.

Thursday Morning, half-past Seven.—Up and dressed and downstairs in order to finish my letter in time for the parcel. At eight I have an appointment with Madame B., who wants to show me something downstairs. At nine we are to set off for Grafton House, and get that over before breakfast. Edward is so kind as to walk there with us. We are to be at Mr. Spence's again at 11.5: from that time shall be driving about I suppose till four o'clock at least. We are, if possible, to call on Mrs. Tilson.

Mr. Hall was very punctual yesterday, and curled me out at a great rate. I thought it looked hideous, and longed for a snug cap instead, but my companions silenced me by their admiration. I had only a bit of velvet round my head. I did not catch cold, however. The weather is all in my favor. I have had no pain in my face since I left you.

We had very good places in the box next the stage-box, front and second row; the three old ones behind, of course. I was particularly disappointed at seeing nothing of Mr. Crabbe. I felt sure of him when I saw that the boxes were fitted up with crimson velvet. The new Mr. Terry was Lord Ogleby, and Henry thinks he may do; but there was no acting more than moderate, and I was as much amused by the remembrances connected with "Midas" as with any part of it. The girls were very much delighted, but still prefer "Don Juan;" and I must say that I have seen nobody on the stage who has been a more interesting character than that compound of cruelty and lust.

It was not possible for me to get the worsteds yesterday. I heard Edward last night pressing Henry to come to you, and I think Henry engaged to go there after his November collection. Nothing has been done as to S. and S.[23] The books came to hand too late for him to have time for it before he went. Mr. Hastings never hinted at Eliza in the smallest degree. Henry knew nothing of Mr. Trimmer's death. I tell you these things that you may not have to ask them over again.

There is a new clerk sent down to Alton, a Mr. Edmund Williams, a young man whom Henry thinks most highly of, and he turns out to be a son of the luckless Williamses of Grosvenor Place.

I long to have you hear Mr. H.'s opinion of P. and P. His admiring my Elizabeth so much is particularly welcome to me.

Instead of saving my superfluous wealth for you to spend, I am going to treat myself with spending it myself. I hope, at least, that I shall find some poplin at Layton and Shear's that will tempt me to buy it. If I do, it shall be sent to Chawton, as half will be for you; for I depend upon your being so kind as to accept it, being the main point. It will be a great pleasure to me. Don't say a word. I only wish you could choose too. I shall send twenty yards.

Now for Bath. Poor F. Cage has suffered a good deal from her accident. The noise of the White Hart was terrible to her. They will keep her quiet, I dare say. She is not so much delighted with the place as the rest of the party; probably, as she says herself, from having been less well, but she thinks she should like it better in the season. The streets are very empty now, and the shops not so gay as she expected. They are at No. 1 Henrietta Street, the corner of Laura Place, and have no acquaintance at present but the Bramstons.

Lady Bridges drinks at the Cross Bath, her son at the Hot, and Louisa is going to bathe. Dr. Parry seems to be half starving Mr. Bridges, for he is restricted to much such a diet as James's, bread, water and meat, and is never to eat so much of that as he wishes, and he is to walk a great deal,—walk till he drops, I believe,—gout or no gout. It really is to that purpose. I have not exaggerated.

Charming weather for you and us, and the travellers, and everybody. You will take your walk this afternoon, and . . .

Henrietta Street, the autumn of 1813.
Miss AUSTEN, Chawton.
By favor of Mr. Gray.

FOOTNOTES:

[20] Eliza, Henry Austen's first wife, who had died in the earlier part of this year.
[21] "Pride and Prejudice."
[22] Lizzy and Marianne.
[23] "Sense and Sensibility."

XLVI.

HENRIETTA STREET,
Thursday (Sept. 16, after dinner),

THANK you, my dearest Cassandra, for the nice long letter I sent off this morning. I hope you have had it by this time, and that it has found you all well, and my mother no more in need of leeches. Whether this will be delivered to you by Henry on Saturday evening, or by the postman on Sunday morning, I know not, as he has lately recollected something of an engagement for Saturday, which perhaps may delay his visit. He seems determined to come to you soon, however.

I hope you will receive the gown to-morrow, and may be able with tolerable honesty to say that you like the color. It was bought at Grafton House, where, by going very early, we got immediate attendance and went on very comfortably. I only forgot the one particular thing which I had always resolved to buy there,—a white silk handkerchief,—and was therefore obliged to give six shillings for one at Crook and Besford's; which reminds me to say that the worsteds ought also to be at Chawton to-morrow, and that I shall be very happy to hear they are approved. I had not much time for deliberation.

We are now all four of us young ladies sitting round the circular table in the inner room writing our letters, while the two brothers are having a comfortable coze in the room adjoining. It is to be a quiet evening, much to the satisfaction of four of the six. My eyes are quite tired of dust and lamps.

The letter you forwarded from Edward, junr., has been duly received. He has been shooting most prosperously at home, and dining at Chilham Castle and with Mr. Scudamore.

My cap is come home, and I like it very much. Fanny has one also; hers is white sarsenet and lace, of a different shape from mine, more fit for morning carriage wear, which is what it is intended for, and is in shape exceedingly like our own satin and lace of last winter; shaped round the face exactly like it, with pipes and more fulness, and a round crown inserted behind. My cap has a peak in front. Large full bows of very narrow ribbon (old twopenny) are the thing. One over the right temple, perhaps, and another at the left ear.

Henry is not quite well. His stomach is rather deranged. You must keep him in rhubarb, and give him plenty of port and water. He caught his cold farther back than I told you,—before he got to Matlock, somewhere in his journey from the North; but the ill effects of that I hope are nearly gone.

We returned from Grafton House only just in time for breakfast, and had scarcely finished breakfast when the carriage came to the door. From eleven to half-past three we were hard at it; we did contrive to get to Hans Place for ten minutes. Mrs. T. was as affectionate and pleasing as ever.

After our return Mr. Tilson walked up from the Compting House and called upon us, and these have been all our visitings.

I have rejoiced more than once that I bought my writing-paper in the country; we have not had a quarter of an hour to spare.

I enclose the eighteen-pence due to my mother. The rose color was 6s. and the other 4s. per yard. There was but two yards and a quarter of the dark slate in the shop, but the man promised to match it and send it off correctly.

Fanny bought her Irish at Newton's in Leicester Square, and I took the opportunity of thinking about your Irish, and seeing one piece of the yard wide at 4s., and it seemed to me very good; good enough for your purpose. It might at least be worth your while to go there, if you have no other engagements. Fanny is very much pleased with the stockings she has bought of Remmington, silk at 12s., cotton at 4s. 3d. She thinks them great bargains, but I have not seen them yet, as my hair was dressing when the man and the stockings came.

The poor girls and their teeth! I have not mentioned them yet, but we were a whole hour at Spence's, and Lizzy's were filed and lamented over again, and poor Marianne had two taken out after all, the two just beyond the eye teeth, to make room for those in front. When her doom was fixed, Fanny, Lizzy, and I walked into the next room, where we heard each of the two sharp and hasty screams.

The little girls' teeth I can suppose in a critical state, but I think he must be a lover of teeth and money and mischief, to parade about Fanny's. I would not have had him look at mine for a shilling a tooth and double it. It was a disagreeable hour.

We then went to Wedgwood's, where my brother and Fanny chose a dinner-set. I believe the pattern is a small lozenge in purple, between lines of narrow gold, and it is to have the crest.

We must have been three-quarters of an hour at Grafton House, Edward sitting by all the time with wonderful patience. There Fanny bought the net for Anna's gown, and a beautiful square veil for herself. The edging there is very cheap. I was tempted by some, and I bought some very nice plaiting lace at 3s. 4d.

Fanny desires me to tell Martha, with her kind love, that Birchall assured her there was no second set of Hook's Lessons for Beginners, and that, by my advice, she has therefore chosen her a set by another composer. I thought she would rather have something than not. It costs six shillings.

With love to you all, including Triggs, I remain,

Yours very affectionately,
J. Austen.

Henrietta St., autumn of 1813.
Miss Austen, Chawton.
By favor of

XLVII.

GODMERSHAM PARK, Thursday (Sept. 23).

MY DEAREST CASSANDRA,—Thank you five hundred and forty times for the exquisite piece of workmanship which was brought into the room this morning, while we were at breakfast, with some very inferior works of art in the same way, and which I read with high glee, much delighted with everything it told, whether good or bad. It is so rich in striking intelligence that I hardly know what to reply to first. I believe finery must have it.

I am extremely glad that you like the poplin. I thought it would have my mother's approbation, but was not so confident of yours. Remember that it is a present. Do not refuse me. I am very rich.

Mrs. Clement is very welcome to her little boy, and to my congratulations into the bargain, if ever you think of giving them. I hope she will do well. Her sister in Lucina, Mrs. H. Gipps, does too well, we think. Mary P. wrote on Sunday that she had been three days on the sofa. Sackree does not approve it.

Well, there is some comfort in the Mrs. Hulbart's not coming to you, and I am happy to hear of the honey. I was thinking of it the other day. Let me know when you begin the new tea and the new white wine. My present elegances have not yet made me indifferent to such matters. I am still a cat if I see a mouse.

I am glad you like our caps, but Fanny is out of conceit with hers already; she finds that she has been buying a new cap without having a new pattern, which is true enough. She is rather out of luck to like neither her gown nor her cap, but I do not much mind it, because besides that I like them both myself, I consider it as a thing of course at her time of life,—one of the sweet taxes of youth to choose in a hurry and make bad bargains.

I wrote to Charles yesterday, and Fanny has had a letter from him to-day, principally to make inquiries about the time of their visit here, to which mine was an answer beforehand; so he will probably write again soon to fix his week. I am best pleased that Cassy does not go to you.

Now, what have we been doing since I wrote last? The Mr. K.'s[24] came a little before dinner on Monday, and Edward went to the church with the two seniors, but there is no inscription yet drawn up. They are very good-natured, you know, and civil, and all that, but are not particularly superfine; however, they ate their dinner and drank their tea, and went away, leaving their lovely Wadham in our arms, and I wish you had seen Fanny and me running backwards and forwards with his breeches from the little chintz to the white room before we went to bed, in the greatest of frights lest he should come upon us before we had done it all. There had been a mistake in the housemaid's preparation, and they were gone to bed.

He seems a very harmless sort of young man, nothing to like or dislike in him,—goes out shooting or hunting with the two others all the morning, and plays at whist and makes queer faces in the evening....

FOOTNOTES:

[24] Knatchbulls.

XLVIII.

GODMERSHAM PARK, Monday (Oct. 11).

[MY DEAREST AUNT CASS.,—I have just asked Aunt Jane to let me write a little in her letter, but she does not like it, so I won't. Good-by!]

You will have Edward's letter to-morrow. He tells me that he did not send you any news to interfere with mine, but I do not think there is much for anybody to send at present.

We had our dinner-party on Wednesday, with the addition of Mrs. and Miss Milles, who were under a promise of dining here in their return from Eastwell, whenever they paid their visit of duty there, and it happened to be paid on that day. Both mother and daughter are much as I have always found them. I like the mother—first, because she reminds me of Mrs. Birch; and, secondly, because she is cheerful and grateful for what she is at the age of ninety and upwards. The day was pleasant enough. I sat by Mr. Chisholme, and we talked away at a great rate about nothing worth hearing.

It was a mistake as to the day of the Sherers going being fixed; they are ready, but are waiting for Mr. Paget's answer.

I inquired of Mrs. Milles after Jemima Brydges, and was quite grieved to hear that she was obliged to leave Canterbury some months ago on account of her debts, and is nobody knows where. What an unprosperous family!

On Saturday, soon after breakfast, Mr. J. P. left us for Norton Court. I like him very much. He gives me the idea of a very amiable young man, only too diffident to be so agreeable as he might be. He was out the chief of each morning with the other two, shooting and getting wet through. To-morrow we are to know whether he and a hundred young ladies will come here for the ball. I do not much expect any.

The Deedes cannot meet us; they have engagements at home. I will finish the Deedes by saying that they are not likely to come here till quite late in my stay,—the very last week perhaps; and I do not expect to see the Moores at all. They are not solicited till after Edward's return from Hampshire.

Monday, November 15, is the day now fixed for our setting out.

Poor Basingstoke races! There seem to have been two particularly wretched days on purpose for them; and Weyhill week does not begin much happier.

We were quite surprised by a letter from Anna at Tollard Royal, last Saturday; but perfectly approve her going, and only regret they should all go so far to stay so few days.

We had thunder and lightning here on Thursday morning, between five and seven; no very bad thunder, but a great deal of lightning. It has given the commencement of a season of wind and rain, and perhaps for the next six weeks we shall not have two dry days together.

Lizzy is very much obliged to you for your letter and will answer it soon, but has so many things to do that it may be four or five days before she can. This is quite her own message, spoken in rather a desponding tone. Your letter gave pleasure to all of us; we had all the reading of it of course,—I three times, as I undertook, to the great relief of Lizzy, to read it to Sackree, and afterwards to Louisa.

Sackree does not at all approve of Mary Doe and her nuts,—on the score of propriety rather than health. She saw some signs of going after her in George and Henry, and thinks if you could give the girl a check, by rather reproving her for taking anything seriously about nuts which they said to her, it might be of use. This, of course, is between our three discreet selves, a scene of triennial bliss.

Mrs. Breton called here on Saturday. I never saw her before.

She is a large, ungenteel woman, with self-satisfied and would-be elegant manners.

We are certain of some visitors to-morrow. Edward Bridges comes for two nights in his way from Lenham to Ramsgate, and brings a friend—name unknown—but supposed to be a Mr. Harpur, a neighboring clergyman; and Mr. R. Mascall is to shoot with the young men, which it is to be supposed will end in his staying dinner.

On Thursday, Mr. Lushington, M.P. for Canterbury, and manager of the Lodge Hounds, dines here, and stays the night. He is chiefly young Edward's acquaintance. If I can I will get a frank from him, and write to you all the sooner. I suppose the Ashford ball will furnish something.

As I wrote of my nephews with a little bitterness in my last, I think it particularly incumbent on me to do them justice now, and I have great pleasure in saying that they were both at the Sacrament yesterday. After having much praised or much blamed anybody, one is generally sensible of something just the reverse soon afterwards. Now these two boys who are out with the foxhounds will come home and disgust me again by some habit of luxury or some proof of sporting mania, unless I keep it off by this prediction. They amuse themselves very comfortably in the evening by netting; they are each about a rabbit net, and sit as deedily to it, side by side, as any two Uncle Franks could do.

I am looking over "Self-Control" again, and my opinion is confirmed of its being an excellently meant, elegantly written work, without anything of nature or probability in it. I declare I do not know whether Laura's passage down the American river is not the most natural, possible, every-day thing she ever does.

Tuesday.—Dear me! what is to become of me? Such a long letter! Two-and-forty lines in the second page. Like Harriot Byron, I ask, what am I to do with my gratitude? I can do nothing but thank you and go on. A few of your inquiries, I think, are replied to *en avance.*

The name of F. Cage's drawing-master is O'Neil. We are

exceedingly amused with your Shalden news, and your self-reproach on the subject of Mrs. Stockwell made me laugh heartily. I rather wondered that Johncock,[25] the only person in the room, could help laughing too. I had not heard before of her having the measles. Mrs. H. and Alethea's staying till Friday was quite new to me; a good plan, however. I could not have settled it better myself, and am glad they found so much in the house to approve, and I hope they will ask Martha to visit them. I admire the sagacity and taste of Charlotte Williams. Those large dark eyes always judge well. I will compliment her by naming a heroine after her.

Edward has had all the particulars of the building, etc., read to him twice over, and seems very well satisfied. A narrow door to the pantry is the only subject of solicitude; it is certainly just the door which should not be narrow, on account of the trays; but if a case of necessity, it must be borne.

I knew there was sugar in the tin, but had no idea of there being enough to last through your company. All the better. You ought not to think this new loaf better than the other, because that was the first of five which all came together. Something of fancy, perhaps, and something of imagination.

Dear Mrs. Digweed! I cannot bear that she should not be foolishly happy after a ball. I hope Miss Yates and her companions were all well the day after their arrival. I am thoroughly rejoiced that Miss Benn has placed herself in lodgings, though I hope they may not be long necessary.

No letter from Charles yet.

Southey's "Life of Nelson." I am tired of "Lives of Nelson," being that I never read any. I will read this, however, if Frank is mentioned in it.

Here am I in Kent, with one brother in the same county and another brother's wife, and see nothing of them, which seems unnatural. It will not last so forever, I trust. I should like to have Mrs. F. A. and her children here for a week, but not a syllable of that nature is ever breathed. I wish her last visit had not been so long a one.

I wonder whether Mrs. Tilson has ever lain-in. Mention it if it ever comes to your knowledge, and we shall hear of it by the same post from Henry.

Mr. Rob. Mascall breakfasted here; he eats a great deal of butter. I dined upon goose yesterday, which, I hope, will secure a good sale of my second edition. Have you any tomatas? Fanny and I regale on them every day.

Disastrous letters from the Plumptres and Oxendens. Refusals everywhere—a blank *partout*—and it is not quite certain whether we go or not; something may depend upon the disposition of Uncle Edward when he comes, and upon what we hear at Chilham Castle this morning, for we are going to pay visits. We are going to each house at Chilham and to Mystole. I shall like seeing the Faggs. I shall like it all, except that we are to set out so early that I have not time to write as I would wish.

Edwd. Bridges's friend is a Mr. Hawker, I find, not Harpur. I would not have you sleep in such an error for the world.

My brother desires his best love and thanks for all your information. He hopes the roots of the old beech have been dug away enough to allow a proper covering of mould and turf. He is sorry for the necessity of building the new coin, but hopes they will contrive that the doorway should be of the usual width,—if it must be contracted on one side, by widening it on the other. The appearance need not signify. And he desires me to say that your being at Chawton when he is will be quite necessary. You cannot think it more indispensable than he does. He is very much obliged to you for your attention to everything. Have you any idea of returning with him to Henrietta Street and finishing your visit then? Tell me your sweet little innocent ideas.

Everything of love and kindness, proper and improper, must now suffice.

Yours very affectionately,
J. AUSTEN.

Miss AUSTEN, Chawton, Alton, Hants.

FOOTNOTE:

[25] The butler at Godmersham.

XLIX.

GODMERSHAM PARK, Thursday (Oct. 14).

MY DEAREST CASSANDRA,—Now I will prepare for Mr. Lushington, and as it will be wisest also to prepare for his not coming, or my not getting a frank, I shall write very close from the first, and even leave room for the seal in the proper place. When I have followed up my last with this I shall feel somewhat less unworthy of you than the state of our correspondence now requires.

I left off in a great hurry to prepare for our morning visits. Of course was ready a good deal the first, and need not have hurried so much. Fanny wore her new gown and cap. I was surprised to find Mystole so pretty.

The ladies were at home. I was in luck, and saw Lady Fagg and all her five daughters, with an old Mrs. Hamilton, from Canterbury, and Mrs. and Miss Chapman, from Margate, into the bargain. I never saw so plain a family,—five sisters so very plain! They are as plain as the Foresters, or the Franfraddops, or the Seagraves, or the Rivers, excluding Sophy. Miss Sally Fagg has a pretty figure, and that comprises all the good looks of the family.

It was stupidish; Fanny did her part very well, but there was a lack of talk altogether, and the three friends in the house only sat by and looked at us. However, Miss Chapman's name is Laura, and she had a double flounce to her gown. You really must get some flounces. Are not some of your large stock of white morning gowns just in a happy state for a flounce—too short? Nobody at home at either house in Chilham.

Edward Bridges and his friend did not forget to arrive. The friend is a Mr. Wigram, one of the three-and-twenty children of a great rich mercantile, Sir Robert Wigram, an old acquaintance of the Footes, but very recently known to Edward B. The history of his coming here is, that, intending to go from Ramsgate to Brighton, Edw. B. persuaded him to take Lenham on his way, which gave him the convenience of Mr. W.'s gig, and the comfort of not being alone there; but, probably thinking a few days of Gm. would be the cheapest and pleasantest way of entertaining his friend and himself, offered a visit here, and here they stay till to-morrow.

Mr. W. is about five or six-and-twenty, not ill-looking, and not agreeable. He is certainly no addition. A sort of cool, gentlemanlike manner, but very silent. They say his name is Henry, a proof how unequally the gifts of fortune are bestowed. I have seen many a John and Thomas much more agreeable.

We have got rid of Mr. R. Mascall, however. I did not like him, either. He talks too much, and is conceited, besides having a vulgarly shaped mouth. He slept here on Tuesday, so that yesterday Fanny and I sat down to breakfast with six gentlemen to admire us.

We did not go to the ball. It was left to her to decide, and at last she determined against it. She knew that it would be a sacrifice on the part of her father and brothers if they went, and I hope it will prove that she has not sacrificed much. It is not likely that there should have been anybody there whom she would care for. I was very glad to be spared the trouble of dressing and going, and being weary before it was half over; so my gown and my cap are still unworn. It will appear at last, perhaps, that I might have done without either. I produced my brown bombazine yesterday, and it was very much admired indeed, and I like it better than ever.

You have given many particulars of the state of Chawton House, but still we want more. Edward wants to be expressly told that all the round tower, etc., is entirely down, and the door from the best room stopped up; he does not know enough of the appearance of things in that quarter.

He heard from Bath yesterday. Lady B. continues very well, and Dr. Parry's opinion is, that while the water agrees with her she ought to remain there, which throws their coming away at a greater uncertainty than we had supposed. It will end, perhaps, in a fit of the gout, which may prevent her coming away. Louisa thinks her mother's being so well may be quite as much owing to her being so much out of doors as to the water. Lady B. is going to try the hot pump, the Cross bath being about to be painted. Louisa is particularly well herself, and thinks the water has been of use to her. She mentioned our inquiries, etc., to Mr. and Mrs. Alex. Evelyn, and had their best compliments and thanks to give in return. Dr. Parry does not expect Mr. E. to last much longer.

Only think of Mrs. Holder's being dead! Poor woman, she has done the only thing in the world she could possibly do to make one cease to abuse her. Now, if you please, Hooper must have it in his power to do more by his uncle. Lucky for the little girl. An Anne Ekins can hardly be so unfit for the care of a child as a Mrs. Holder.

A letter from Wrotham yesterday offering an early visit here, and Mr. and Mrs. Moore and one child are to come on Monday for ten days. I hope Charles and Fanny may not fix the same time, but if they come at all in October they must. What is the use of hoping? The two parties of children is the chief evil.

To be sure, here we are; the very thing has happened, or rather worse,—a letter from Charles this very morning, which gives us reason to suppose they may come here to-day. It depends upon the weather, and the weather now is very fine. No difficulties are made, however, and, indeed, there will be no want of room; but I wish there were no Wigrams and Lushingtons in the way to fill up the table and make us such a motley set. I cannot spare Mr. Lushington either, because of his frank, but Mr. Wigram does no good to anybody. I cannot imagine how a man can have the impudence to come into a family party for three days, where he is quite a stranger, unless he knows himself to be agreeable on undoubted authority. He and Edw. B. are going to ride to Eastwell, and as the boys are hunting, and my brother is gone to Canty., Fanny and I have a quiet morning before us.

Edward has driven off poor Mrs. Salkeld. It was thought a good opportunity of doing something towards clearing the house. By her own desire Mrs. Fanny[26] is to be put in the room next the nursery, her baby in a little bed by her; and as Cassy is to have the closet within, and Betsey William's little hole, they will be all very snug together. I shall be most happy to see dear Charles, and he will be as happy as he can with a cross child, or some such care, pressing on him at the time. I should be very happy in the idea of seeing little Cassy again, too, did not I fear she would disappoint me by some immediate disagreeableness....

The comfort of the billiard-table here is very great; it draws all the gentlemen to it whenever they are within, especially after dinner, so that my brother, Fanny, and I have the library to ourselves in delightful quiet. There is no truth in the report of G. Hatton being to marry Miss Wemyss. He desires it may be contradicted.

Have you done anything about our present to Miss Benn? I suppose she must have a bed at my mother's whenever she dines there. How will they manage as to inviting her when you are gone? and if they invite, how will they continue to entertain her?

Let me know as many of your parting arrangements as you can, as to wine, etc. I wonder whether the ink-bottle has been filled. Does butcher's meat keep up at the same price, and is not bread lower than 2s. 6d.? Mary's blue gown! My mother must be in agonies. I have a great mind to have my blue gown dyed some time or other. I proposed it once to you, and you made some objection, I forget what. It is the fashion of flounces that gives it particular expediency.

Mrs. and Miss Wildman have just been here. Miss is very plain. I wish Lady B. may be returned before we leave Gm., that Fanny may spend the time of her father's absence at Goodnestone, which is what she would prefer.

Friday.—They came last night at about seven. We had given them up, but I still expected them to come. Dessert was nearly over; a better time for arriving than an hour and a half earlier. They were late because they did not set out earlier, and did not allow time enough. Charles did not aim at more than reaching Sittingbourne by three, which could not have brought them here by dinner-time. They had a very rough passage; he would not have ventured if he had known how bad it would be.

However, here they are, safe and well, just like their own nice selves, Fanny looking as neat and white this morning as possible, and dear Charles all affectionate, placid, quiet, cheerful good-humor. They are both looking very well, but poor little Cassy is grown extremely thin, and looks poorly. I hope a week's country air and exercise may do her good. I am sorry to say it can be but a week. The baby does not appear so large in proportion as she was, nor quite so pretty, but I have seen very little of her. Cassy was too tired and bewildered just at first to seem to know anybody. We met them in the hall—the women and girl part of us—but before we reached the library she kissed me very affectionately, and has since seemed to recollect me in the same way.

It was quite an evening of confusion, as you may suppose. At first we were all walking about from one part of the house to the other; then came a fresh dinner in the breakfast-room for Charles and his wife, which Fanny and I attended; then we moved into the library, were joined by the dining-room people, were introduced, and so forth; and then we had tea and coffee, which was not over till past ten. Billiards again drew all the odd ones away; and Edward, Charles, the two Fannies, and I sat snugly talking. I shall be glad to have our numbers a little reduced, and by the time you receive this we shall be only a family, though a large family, party. Mr. Lushington goes to-morrow.

Now I must speak of him, and I like him very much. I am sure he is clever, and a man of taste. He got a volume of Milton last night, and spoke of it with warmth. He is quite an M. P., very smiling, with an exceeding good address and readiness of language. I am rather in love with him. I dare say he is ambitious and insincere. He puts me in mind of Mr. Dundas. He has a wide smiling mouth, and very good teeth, and something the same complexion and nose. He is a much shorter man, with Martha's leave. Does Martha never hear from Mrs. Craven? Is Mrs. Craven never at home?

We breakfasted in the dining-room to-day, and are now all pretty well dispersed and quiet. Charles and George are gone out shooting together, to Winnigates and Seaton Wood. I asked on purpose to tell Henry. Mr. Lushington and Edwd. are gone some other way. I wish Charles may kill something; but this high wind is against their sport.

Lady Williams is living at the Rose at Sittingbourne; they called upon her yesterday; she cannot live at Sheerness, and as soon as she gets to Sittingbourne is quite well. In return for all your matches, I announce that her brother William is going to marry a Miss Austen, of a Wiltshire family, who say they are related to us.

I talk to Cassy about Chawton; she remembers much, but does not volunteer on the subject. Poor little love! I wish she were not so very Palmery, but it seems stronger than ever. I never knew a wife's family features have such undue influence.

Papa and mamma have not yet made up their mind as to parting with her or not; the chief, indeed the only, difficulty with mamma is a very reasonable one, the child's being very unwilling to leave them. When it was mentioned to her she did not like the idea of it at all. At the same time she has been suffering so much lately from sea-sickness that her mamma cannot bear to have her much on board this winter. Charles is less inclined to part with her. I do not know how it will end, or what is to determine it. He desires his best love to you, and has not written because he has not been able to decide. They are both very sensible of your kindness on the occasion.

I have made Charles furnish me with something to say about

young Kendall. He is going on very well. When he first joined the "Namur," my brother did not find him forward enough to be what they call put in the office, and therefore placed him under the schoolmaster; but he is very much improved, and goes into the office now every afternoon, still attending school in the morning.

This cold weather comes very fortunately for Edward's nerves, with such a house full; it suits him exactly; he is all alive and cheerful. Poor James, on the contrary, must be running his toes into the fire. I find that Mary Jane Fowle was very near returning with her brother and paying them a visit on board. I forget exactly what hindered her; I believe the Cheltenham scheme. I am glad something did. They are to go to Cheltenham on Monday se'nnight. I don't vouch for their going, you know; it only comes from one of the family.

Now I think I have written you a good-sized letter, and may deserve whatever I can get in reply. Infinities of love. I must distinguish that of Fanny, senior, who particularly desires to be remembered to you all.

Yours very affectionately,
J. AUSTEN.

FAVERSHAM, Oct. 15, 1813.
Miss AUSTEN, Chawton, Alton, Hants.
Per S. R. LUSHINGTON.

FOOTNOTE:

[26] Mrs. Charles Austen, *née* Fanny Palmer.

L.

GODMERSHAM PARK, Oct. 18.

MY DEAR AUNT CASSANDRA,—I am very much obliged to you for your long letter and for the nice account of Chawton. We are all very glad to hear that the Adams are gone, and hope Dame Libscombe will be more happy now with her deaffy child, as she calls it, but I am afraid there is not much chance of her remaining long sole mistress of her house.

I am sorry you had not any better news to send us of our hare, poor little thing! I thought it would not live long in that *Pondy House*; I don't wonder that Mary Doe is very sorry it is dead, because we promised her that if it was alive when we came back to Chawton, we would reward her for her trouble.

Papa is much obliged to you for ordering the scrubby firs to be cut down; I think he was rather frightened at first about the great oak. Fanny quite believed it, for she exclaimed, "Dear me, what a pity, how could they be so stupid!" I hope by this time they have put up some hurdles for the sheep, or turned out the cart-horses from the lawn.

Pray tell grandmamma that we have begun getting seeds for her; I hope we shall be able to get her a nice collection, but I am afraid this wet weather is very much against them. How glad I am to hear she has had such good success with her chickens, but I wish there had been more bantams amongst them. I am very sorry to hear of poor Lizzie's fate.

I must now tell you something about our poor people. I believe you know old Mary Croucher; she gets *maderer* and *maderer* every day. Aunt Jane has been to see her, but it was on one of her rational days. Poor Will Amos hopes your skewers are doing well; he has left his house in the poor Row, and lives in a barn at Builting. We asked him why he went away, and he said the fleas were so starved when he came back from Chawton that they all flew upon him and *eenermost* eat him up.

How unlucky it is that the weather is so wet! Poor Uncle Charles has come home half drowned every day.

I don't think little Fanny is quite so pretty as she was; one reason is because she wears short petticoats, I believe. I hope Cook is better; she was very unwell the day we went away. Papa has given me half-a-dozen new pencils, which are very good ones indeed; I draw every other day. I hope you go and whip Lucy Chalcraft every night.

Miss Clewes begs me to give her very best respects to you; she is very much obliged to you for your kind inquiries after her. Pray give my duty to grandmamma and love to Miss Floyd. I remain, my dear Aunt Cassandra, your very affectionate niece,

ELIZTH. KNIGHT.

Thursday.—I think Lizzy's letter will entertain you. Thank you for yours just received. To-morrow shall be fine if possible. You will be at Guildford before our party set off. They only go to Key Street, as Mr. Street the Purser lives there, and they have promised to dine and sleep with him.

Cassy's looks are much mended. She agrees pretty well with her cousins, but is not quite happy among them; they are too many and too boisterous for her. I have given her your message, but she said nothing, and did not look as if the idea of going to Chawton again was a pleasant one. They have Edward's carriage to Ospringe.

I think I have just done a good deed,—extracted Charles from his wife and children upstairs, and made him get ready to go out shooting, and not keep Mr. Moore waiting any longer.

Mr. and Mrs. Sherer and Joseph dined here yesterday very

prettily. Edw. and Geo. were absent,—gone for a night to Eastling. The two Fannies went to Canty. in the morning, and took Lou. and Cass. to try on new stays. Harriet and I had a comfortable walk together. She desires her best love to you and kind remembrance to Henry. Fanny's best love also. I fancy there is to be another party to Canty. to-morrow,—Mr. and Mrs. Moore and me.

Edward thanks Henry for his letter. We are most happy to hear he is so much better. I depend upon you for letting me know what he wishes as to my staying with him or not; you will be able to find out, I dare say. I had intended to beg you would bring one of my nightcaps with you, in case of my staying, but forgot it when I wrote on Tuesday. Edward is much concerned about his pond; he cannot now doubt the fact of its running out, which he was resolved to do as long as possible.

I suppose my mother will like to have me write to her. I shall try at least.

No; I have never seen the death of Mrs. Crabbe. I have only just been making out from one of his prefaces that he probably was married. It is almost ridiculous. Poor woman! I will comfort him as well as I can, but I do not undertake to be good to her children. She had better not leave any.

Edw. and Geo. set off this day week for Oxford. Our party will then be very small, as the Moores will be going about the same time. To enliven us, Fanny proposes spending a few days soon afterwards at Fredville. It will really be a good opportunity, as her father will have a companion. We shall all three go to Wrotham, but Edwd. and I stay only a night perhaps. Love to Mr. Tilson.

Yours very affectionately,
J. A.

Miss AUSTEN,
10 Henrietta St., Covent Garden, London.

LI.

GODMERSHAM PARK, Wednesday (Nov. 3).

MY DEAREST CASSANDRA,—I will keep this celebrated birthday by writing to you; and as my pen seems inclined to write large, I will put my lines very close together. I had but just time to enjoy your letter yesterday before Edward and I set off in the chair for Canty., and I allowed him to hear the chief of it as we went along.

We rejoice sincerely in Henry's gaining ground as he does, and hope there will be weather for him to get out every day this week, as the likeliest way of making him equal to what he plans for the next. If he is tolerably well, the going into Oxfordshire will make him better, by making him happier.

Can it be that I have not given you the minutiæ of Edward's plans? See, here they are: To go to Wrotham on Saturday the 13th, spend Sunday there, and be in town on Monday to dinner, and if agreeable to Henry, spend one whole day with him, which day is likely to be Tuesday, and so go down to Chawton on Wednesday.

But now I cannot be quite easy without staying a little while with Henry, unless he wishes it otherwise; his illness and the dull time of year together make me feel that it would be horrible of me not to offer to remain with him, and therefore unless you know of any objection, I wish you would tell him with my best love that I shall be most happy to spend ten days or a fortnight in Henrietta St., if he will accept me. I do not offer more than a fortnight, because I shall then have been some time from home; but it will be a great pleasure to be with him, as it always is. I have the less regret and scruple on your account, because I shall see you for a day and a half, and because you will have Edward for at least a week. My scheme is to take Bookham in my way home for a few days, and my hope that Henry will be so good as to send me some part of the way thither. I have a most kind repetition of Mrs. Cooke's two or three dozen invitations, with the offer of meeting me anywhere in one of her airings.

Fanny's cold is much better. By dosing and keeping her room on Sunday, she got rid of the worst of it, but I am rather afraid of what this day may do for her; she is gone to Canty. with Miss Clewes, Liz., and Marnne, and it is but roughish weather for any one in a tender state. Miss Clewes has been going to Canty. ever since her return, and it is now just accomplishing.

Edward and I had a delightful morning for our drive there, I enjoyed it thoroughly; but the day turned off before we were ready, and we came home in some rain and the apprehension of a great deal. It has not done us any harm, however. He went to inspect the gaol, as a visiting magistrate, and took me with him. I was gratified, and went through all the feelings which people must go through, I think, in visiting such a building. We paid no other visits, only walked about snugly together, and shopped. I bought a concert ticket and a sprig of flowers for my old age.

To vary the subject from gay to grave with inimitable address, I shall now tell you something of the Bath party—and still a Bath party they are, for a fit of the gout came on last week. The accounts of Lady B. are as good as can be under such a circumstance; Dr. P. says it appears a good sort of gout, and her spirits are better than usual, but as to her coming away, it is of course all uncertainty. I have very little doubt of Edward's going down to Bath, if they have not left it when he is in Hampshire; if he does, he will go on from Steventon, and then return direct to London, without coming back to Chawton. This detention does not suit his feelings. It may be rather a good thing, however, that Dr. P. should see Lady B. with the gout on her. Harriot was quite wishing for it.

The day seems to improve. I wish my pen would too.

Sweet Mr. Ogle! I dare say he sees all the panoramas for nothing, has free admittance everywhere; he is so delightful! Now, you need not see anybody else.

I am glad to hear of our being likely to have a peep at Charles and Fanny at Christmas, but do not force poor Cass. to stay if she hates it. You have done very right as to Mrs. F. A. Your tidings of S. and S. give me pleasure. I have never seen it advertised.

Harriot, in a letter to Fanny to-day, inquires whether they sell cloths for pelisses at Bedford House, and, if they do, will be very much obliged to you to desire them to send her down patterns, with the width and prices; they may go from Charing Cross almost any day in the week, but if it is a ready-money house it will not do, for the *bru* of *feu* the Archbishop says she cannot pay for it immediately. Fanny and I suspect they do not deal in the article.

The Sherers, I believe, are now really going to go; Joseph has had a bed here the last two nights, and I do not know whether this is not the day of moving. Mrs. Sherer called yesterday to take leave. The weather looks worse again.

We dine at Chilham Castle to-morrow, and I expect to find some amusement, but more from the concert the next day, as I am sure of seeing several that I want to see. We are to meet a party from Goodnestone, Lady B., Miss Hawley, and Lucy Foote, and I am to meet Mrs. Harrison, and we are to talk about Ben and Anna. "My dear Mrs. Harrison," I shall say, "I am afraid the young man has some of your family madness; and though there often appears to be something of madness in Anna too, I think she inherits more of it from her mother's family than from ours." That is what I shall say, and I think she will find it difficult to answer me.

I took up your letter again to refresh me, being somewhat tired, and was struck with the prettiness of the hand: it is really a very pretty hand now and then,—so small and so neat! I wish I could get as much into a sheet of paper.[27] Another time I will take two days to make a letter in: it is fatiguing to write a whole long one at once. I hope to hear from you again on Sunday and again on Friday, the day before we move. On Monday, I suppose, you will be going to Streatham, to see quiet Mr. Hill and eat very bad baker's bread.

A fall in bread by the by. I hope my mother's bill next week will show it. I have had a very comfortable letter from her, one of her foolscap sheets quite full of little home news. Anna was there the first of the two days. An Anna sent away and an Anna fetched are different things. This will be an excellent time for Ben to pay his visit, now that we, the formidables, are absent.

I did not mean to eat, but Mr. Johncock has brought in the tray, so I must. I am all alone. Edward is gone into his woods. At this present time I have five tables, eight-and-twenty chairs, and two fires all to myself.

Miss Clewes is to be invited to go to the concert with us; there will be my brother's place and ticket for her, as he cannot go. He and the other connections of the Cages are to meet at Milgate that very day, to consult about a proposed alteration of the Maidstone road, in which the Cages are very much interested. Sir Brook comes here in the morning, and they are to be joined by Mr. Deedes at Ashford. The loss of the concert will be no great evil to the Squire. We shall be a party of three ladies therefore, and to meet three ladies.

What a convenient carriage Henry's is, to his friends in general! Who has it next? I am glad William's going is voluntary, and on no worse grounds. An inclination for the country is a venial fault. He has more of Cowper than of Johnson in him,— fonder of tame hares and blank verse than of the full tide of human existence at Charing Cross.

Oh! I have more of such sweet flattery from Miss Sharp. She is an excellent kind friend. I am read and admired in Ireland too. There is a Mrs. Fletcher, the wife of a judge, an old lady, and very good and very clever, who is all curiosity to know about me,— what I am like, and so forth. I am not known to her by name, however. This comes through Mrs. Carrick, not through Mrs.

Gore. You are quite out there.

I do not despair of having my picture in the Exhibition at last,—all white and red, with my head on one side; or perhaps I may marry young Mr. D'Arblay. I suppose in the mean time I shall owe dear Henry a great deal of money for printing, etc.

I hope Mrs. Fletcher will indulge herself with S. and S. If I am to stay in H. S., and if you should be writing home soon, I wish you would be so good as to give a hint of it, for I am not likely to write there again these ten days, having written yesterday.

Fanny has set her heart upon its being a Mr. Brett who is going to marry a Miss Dora Best, of this country. I dare say Henry has no objection. Pray, where did the boys sleep?

The Deedes come here on Monday to stay till Friday, so that we shall end with a flourish the last canto. They bring Isabella and one of the grown-ups, and will come in for a Canty. ball on Thursday. I shall be glad to see them. Mrs. Deedes and I must talk rationally together, I suppose.

Edward does not write to Henry, because of my writing so often. God bless you. I shall be so glad to see you again, and I wish you many happy returns of this day. Poor Lord Howard! How he does cry about it!

Yours very truly,

J. A.

Miss AUSTEN,
10 Henrietta Street, Covent Garden, London.

FOOTNOTE:

[27] I cannot pass this paragraph over without remarking that it is hardly possible to imagine anything neater or prettier than Jane's own hand. Most of her letters are beautifully written, and the MS. of her "Lady Susan" remarkably so.—*Note by Lord* BRABOURNE.

LII.

GODMERSHAM PARK, Saturday (Nov. 6).

MY DEAREST CASSANDRA,—Having half an hour before breakfast (very snug, in my own room, lovely morning, excellent fire—fancy me!) I will give you some account of the last two days. And yet, what is there to be told? I shall get foolishly minute unless I cut the matter short.

We met only the Bretons at Chilham Castle, besides a Mr. and Mrs. Osborne and a Miss Lee staying in the house, and were only fourteen altogether. My brother and Fanny thought it the pleasantest party they had ever known there, and I was very well entertained by bits and scraps. I had long wanted to see Dr. Breton, and his wife amuses me very much with her affected refinement and elegance. Miss Lee I found very conversable; she admires Crabbe as she ought. She is at an age of reason, ten years older than myself at least. She was at the famous ball at Chilham Castle, so of course you remember her.

By the by, as I must leave off being young, I find many *douceurs* in being a sort of *chaperon*, for I am put on the sofa near the fire, and can drink as much wine as I like. We had music in the evening: Fanny and Miss Wildman played, and Mr. James Wildman sat close by and listened, or pretended to listen.

Yesterday was a day of dissipation all through: first came Sir Brook to dissipate us before breakfast; then there was a call from Mr. Sherer, then a regular morning visit from Lady Honeywood in her way home from Eastwell; then Sir Brook and Edward set off; then we dined (five in number) at half-past four; then we had coffee; and at six Miss Clewes, Fanny, and I drove away. We had a beautiful night for our frisks. We were earlier than we need have been, but after a time Lady B. and her two companions appeared,—we had kept places for them; and there we sat, all six in a row, under a side wall, I between Lucy Foote and Miss Clewes.

Lady B. was much what I expected; I could not determine whether she was rather handsome or very plain. I liked her for being in a hurry to have the concert over and get away, and for getting away at last with a great deal of decision and promptness, not waiting to compliment and dawdle and fuss about seeing dear Fanny, who was half the evening in another part of the room with her friends the Plumptres. I am growing too minute, so I will go to breakfast.

When the concert was over, Mrs. Harrison and I found each other out, and had a very comfortable little complimentary friendly chat. She is a sweet woman,—still quite a sweet woman in herself, and so like her sister! I could almost have thought I was speaking to Mrs. Lefroy. She introduced me to her daughter, whom I think pretty, but most dutifully inferior to *la Mère Beauté*. The Faggs and the Hammonds were there,—Wm. Hammond the only young man of renown. Miss looked very handsome, but I prefer her little smiling flirting sister Julia.

I was just introduced at last to Mary Plumptre, but I should hardly know her again. She was delighted with me, however, good enthusiastic soul! And Lady B. found me handsomer than she expected, so you see I am not so very bad as you might think for.

It was twelve before we reached home. We were all dog-tired, but pretty well to-day: Miss Clewes says she has not caught cold, and Fanny's does not seem worse. I was so tired that I began to wonder how I should get through the ball next Thursday; but there will be so much more variety then in walking about, and probably so much less heat, that perhaps I may not feel it more. My china crape is still kept for the ball. Enough of the concert.

I had a letter from Mary yesterday. They travelled down to Cheltenham last Monday very safely, and are certainly to be there a month. Bath is still Bath. The H. Bridges must quit them early next week, and Louisa seems not quite to despair of their all moving together, but to those who see at a distance there appears no chance of it. Dr. Parry does not want to keep Lady B. at Bath when she can once move. That is lucky. You will see poor Mr. Evelyn's death.

Since I wrote last, my 2nd edit. has stared me in the face. Mary tells me that Eliza means to buy it. I wish she may. It can hardly depend upon any more Fyfield Estates. I cannot help hoping that many will feel themselves obliged to buy it. I shall not mind imagining it a disagreeable duty to them, so as they do it. Mary heard before she left home that it was very much admired at Cheltenham, and that it was given to Miss Hamilton. It is pleasant to have such a respectable writer named. I cannot tire you, I am sure, on this subject, or I would apologize.

What weather, and what news! We have enough to do to admire them both. I hope you derive your full share of enjoyment from each.

I have extended my lights and increased my acquaintance a good deal within these two days. Lady Honeywood you know; I did not sit near enough to be a perfect judge, but I thought her extremely pretty, and her manners have all the recommendations of ease and good-humor and unaffectedness; and going about with four horses and nicely dressed herself, she is altogether a perfect sort of woman.

Oh, and I saw Mr. Gipps last night,—the useful Mr. Gipps, whose attentions came in as acceptably to us in handing us to the carriage, for want of a better man, as they did to Emma Plumptre. I thought him rather a good-looking little man.

I long for your letter to-morrow, particularly that I may know my fate as to London. My first wish is that Henry should really choose what he likes best; I shall certainly not be sorry if he does not want me. Morning church to-morrow; I shall come back with impatient feelings.

The Sherers are gone, but the Pagets are not come: we shall therefore have Mr. S. again. Mr. Paget acts like an unsteady man. Dr. Hant, however, gives him a very good character; what is wrong is to be imputed to the lady. I dare say the house likes female government.

I have a nice long black and red letter from Charles, but not communicating much that I did not know.

There is some chance of a good ball next week, as far as females go. Lady Bridges may perhaps be there with some Knatchbulls. Mrs. Harrison perhaps, with Miss Oxenden and the Miss Papillons; and if Mrs. Harrison, then Lady Fagg will come.

The shades of evening are descending, and I resume my interesting narrative. Sir Brook and my brother came back about four, and Sir Brook almost immediately set forward again to Goodnestone. We are to have Edwd. B. to-morrow, to pay us another Sunday's visit,—the last, for more reasons than one; they all come home on the same day that we go. The Deedes do not come till Tuesday; Sophia is to be the comer. She is a disputable beauty that I want much to see. Lady Eliz. Hatton and Annamaria called here this morning. Yes, they called; but I do not think I can say anything more about them. They came, and they sat, and they went.

Sunday.—Dearest Henry! What a turn he has for being ill, and what a thing bile is! This attack has probably been brought on in part by his previous confinement and anxiety; but, however it came, I hope it is going fast, and that you will be able to send a very good account of him on Tuesday. As I hear on Wednesday, of course I shall not expect to hear again on Friday. Perhaps a letter to Wrotham would not have an ill effect.

We are to be off on Saturday before the post comes in, as Edward takes his own horses all the way. He talks of nine o'clock. We shall bait at Lenham.

Excellent sweetness of you to send me such a nice long letter; it made its appearance, with one from my mother, soon after I and my impatient feelings walked in. How glad I am that I did what I did! I was only afraid that you might think the offer superfluous, but you have set my heart at ease. Tell Henry that I will stay with him, let it be ever so disagreeable to him.

Oh, dear me! I have not time on paper for half that I want to say. There have been two letters from Oxford,—one from George yesterday. They got there very safely,—Edwd. two hours behind the coach, having lost his way in leaving London. George writes cheerfully and quietly; hopes to have Utterson's rooms soon; went to lecture on Wednesday, states some of his expenses, and concludes with saying, "I am afraid I shall be poor." I am glad he thinks about it so soon. I believe there is no private tutor yet chosen, but my brother is to hear from Edwd. on the subject shortly.

You, and Mrs. H., and Catherine, and Alethea going about together in Henry's carriage seeing sights—I am not used to the idea of it yet. All that you are to see of Streatham, seen already! Your Streatham and my Bookham may go hang. The prospect of being taken down to Chawton by Henry perfects the plan to me. I was in hopes of your seeing some illuminations, and you have seen them. "I thought you would come, and you did come." I am sorry he is not to come from the Baltic sooner. Poor Mary!

My brother has a letter from Louisa to-day of an unwelcome nature; they are to spend the winter at Bath. It was just decided on. Dr. Parry wished it, not from thinking the water necessary to Lady B., but that he might be better able to judge how far his treatment of her, which is totally different from anything she had been used to, is right; and I suppose he will not mind having a few more of her Ladyship's guineas. His system is a lowering one. He took twelve ounces of blood from her when the gout appeared, and forbids wine, etc. Hitherto the plan agrees with her. She is very well satisfied to stay, but it is a sore disappointment to Louisa and Fanny.

The H. Bridges leave them on Tuesday, and they mean to move into a smaller house; you may guess how Edward feels. There can be no doubt of his going to Bath now; I should not wonder if he brought Fanny Cage back with him.

You shall hear from me once more, some day or other.

Yours very affectionately,
J. A.

We do not like Mr. Hampson's scheme.

Miss AUSTEN,
10 Henrietta Street, Covent Garden, London.

LIII.

We had altogether a very good journey, and everything at Cobham was comfortable. I could not pay Mr. Harrington! That was the only alas! of the business. I shall therefore return his bill, and my mother's 2*l*., that you may try your luck. We did not begin reading till Bentley Green. Henry's approbation is hitherto even equal to my wishes. He says it is different from the other two, but does not appear to think it at all inferior. He has only married Mrs. R.[28] I am afraid he has gone through the most entertaining part. He took to Lady B. and Mrs. N.[29] most kindly, and gives great praise to the drawing of the characters. He understands them all, likes Fanny, and, I think, foresees how it will all be. I finished the "Heroine" last night, and was very much amused by it. I wonder James did not like it better. It diverted me exceedingly. We went to bed at ten. I was very tired, but slept to a miracle, and am lovely to-day, and at present Henry seems to have no complaint. We left Cobham at half-past eight, stopped to bait and breakfast at Kingston, and were in this house considerably before two. Nice smiling Mr. Barlowe met us at the door, and, in reply to inquiries after news, said that peace was generally expected. I have taken possession of my bedroom, unpacked my bandbox, sent Miss P.'s two letters to the twopenny post, been visited by Md. B., and am now writing by myself at the new table in the front room. It is snowing. We had some snowstorms yesterday, and a smart frost at night, which gave us a hard road from Cobham to Kingston; but as it was then getting dirty and heavy, Henry had a pair of leaders put on to the bottom of Sloane St. His own horses, therefore, cannot have had hard work. I watched for veils as we drove through the streets, and had the pleasure of seeing several upon vulgar heads. And now, how do you all do?—you in particular, after the worry of yesterday and the day before. I hope Martha had a pleasant visit again, and that you and my mother could eat your beef-pudding. Depend upon my thinking of the chimney-sweeper as soon as I wake to-morrow. Places are secured at Drury Lane for Saturday, but so great is the rage for seeing Kean that only a third and fourth row could be got; as it is in a front box, however, I hope we shall do pretty well—Shylock, a good play for Fanny—she cannot be much affected, I think. Mrs. Perigord has just been here. She tells me that we owe her master for the silk-dyeing. My poor old muslin has never been dyed yet. It has been promised to be done several times. What wicked people dyers are! They begin with dipping their own souls in scarlet sin. It is evening. We have drank tea, and I have torn through the third vol. of the "Heroine." I do not think it falls off. It is a delightful burlesque, particularly on the Radcliffe style. Henry is going on with "Mansfield Park." He admires H. Crawford: I mean properly, as a clever, pleasant man. I tell you all the good I can, as I know how much you will enjoy it. We hear that Mr. Kean is more admired than ever. There are no good places to be got in Drury Lane for the next fortnight, but Henry means to secure some for Saturday fortnight, when you are reckoned upon. Give my love to little Cass. I hope she found my bed comfortable last night. I have seen nobody in London yet with such a long chin as Dr. Syntax, nor anybody quite so large as Gogmagolicus.

Yours affly,
J. AUSTEN.

FOOTNOTES:
[28] Mrs. Rushworth in "Mansfield Park."
[29] Lady Bertram and Mrs. Norris.

LIV.

HENRIETTA ST., Wednesday (March 9).

WELL, we went to the play again last night, and as we were out a great part of the morning too, shopping, and seeing the Indian jugglers, I am very glad to be quiet now till dressing-time. We are to dine at the Tilsons', and to-morrow at Mr. Spencer's.

We had not done breakfast yesterday when Mr. J. Plumptre appeared to say that he had secured a box. Henry asked him to dine here, which I fancy he was very happy to do, and so at five o'clock we four sat down to table together, while the master of the house was preparing for going out himself. The "Farmer's Wife" is a musical thing in three acts, and as Edward was steady in not staying for anything more, we were at home before ten.

Fanny and Mr. J. P. are delighted with Miss S., and her merit in singing is, I dare say, very great; that she gave me no pleasure is no reflection upon her, nor, I hope, upon myself, being what Nature made me on that article. All that I am sensible of in Miss S. is a pleasing person and no skill in acting. We had Mathews, Liston, and Emery; of course, some amusement.

Our friends were off before half-past eight this morning, and had the prospect of a heavy cold journey before them. I think they both liked their visit very much. I am sure Fanny did. Henry sees decided attachment between her and his new acquaintance.

I have a cold, too, as well as my mother and Martha. Let it be a generous emulation between us which can get rid of it first.

I wear my gauze gown to-day, long sleeves and all. I shall see how they succeed, but as yet I have no reason to suppose long sleeves are allowable. I have lowered the bosom, especially at the corners, and plaited black satin ribbon round the top. Such will be my costume of vine-leaves and paste.

Prepare for a play the very first evening, I rather think Covent Garden, to see Young in "Richard." I have answered for your little companion's being conveyed to Keppel St. immediately. I have never yet been able to get there myself, but hope I shall soon.

What cruel weather this is! and here is Lord Portsmouth married, too, to Miss Hanson.[30]

Henry has finished "Mansfield Park," and his approbation has not lessened. He found the last half of the last volume extremely interesting.

I suppose my mother recollects that she gave me no money for paying Brecknell and Twining, and my funds will not supply enough.

We are home in such good time that I can finish my letter to-night, which will be better than getting up to do it to-morrow, especially as, on account of my cold, which has been very heavy in my head this evening, I rather think of lying in bed later than usual. I would not but be well enough to go to Hertford St. on any account.

We met only Genl. Chowne to-day, who has not much to say for himself. I was ready to laugh at the remembrance of Frederick, and such a different Frederick as we chose to fancy him to the real Christopher!

Mrs. Tilson had long sleeves, too, and she assured me that they are worn in the evening by many. I was glad to hear this. She dines here, I believe, next Tuesday.

On Friday we are to be snug with only Mr. Barlowe and an evening of business. I am so pleased that the mead is brewed. Love to all. I have written to Mrs. Hill, and care for nobody.

Yours affectionately,
J. AUSTEN.

Miss AUSTEN, Chawton.
By favor of Mr. GRAY.

FOOTNOTE:

[30] His second wife. He died in 1853, and was succeeded by his brother, the father of the present earl.

LV.

CHAWTON, Tuesday (June 13).

MY DEAREST CASSANDRA,—Fanny takes my mother to Alton this morning, which gives me an opportunity of sending you a few lines without any other trouble than that of writing them.

This is a delightful day in the country, and I hope not much too hot for town. Well, you had a good journey, I trust, and all that, and not rain enough to spoil your bonnet. It appeared so likely to be a wet evening that I went up to the Gt. House between three and four, and dawdled away an hour very comfortably, though Edwd. was not very brisk. The air was clearer in the evening, and he was better. We all five walked together into the kitchen garden and along the Gosport road, and they drank tea with us.

You will be glad to hear that G. Turner has another situation, something in the cow line, near Rumsey, and he wishes to move immediately, which is not likely to be inconvenient to anybody.

The new nurseryman at Alton comes this morning to value the crops in the garden.

The only letter to-day is from Mrs. Cooke to me. They do not leave home till July, and want me to come to them, according to my promise. And, after considering everything, I have resolved on going. My companions promote it. I will not go, however, till after Edward is gone, that he may feel he has a somebody to give memorandums to, to the last. I must give up all help from his carriage, of course. And, at any rate, it must be such an excess of expense that I have quite made up my mind to it, and do not mean to care.

I have been thinking of Triggs and the chair, you may be sure, but I know it will end in posting. They will meet me at Guildford.

In addition to their standing claims on me they admire "Mansfield Park" exceedingly. Mr. Cooke says "it is the most sensible novel he ever read," and the manner in which I treat the clergy delights them very much. Altogether, I must go, and I want you to join me there when your visit in Henrietta St. is over. Put this into your capacious head.

Take care of yourself, and do not be trampled to death in running after the Emperor. The report in Alton yesterday was that they would certainly travel this road either to or from Portsmouth. I long to know what this bow of the Prince's will produce.

I saw Mrs. Andrews yesterday. Mrs. Browning had seen her before. She is very glad to send an Elizabeth.

Miss Benn continues the same. Mr. Curtis, however, saw her yesterday, and said her hand was going on as well as possible. Accept our best love.

Yours very affectionately,
J. AUSTEN.

Miss AUSTEN, 10 Henrietta Street,
By favor of Mr. GRAY.

LVI.

THURSDAY (June 23).

DEAREST CASSANDRA,—I received your pretty letter while the children were drinking tea with us, as Mr. Louch was so obliging as to walk over with it. Your good account of everybody made us very happy.

I heard yesterday from Frank. When he began his letter he hoped to be here on Monday, but before it was ended he had been told that the naval review would not take place till Friday, which would probably occasion him some delay, as he cannot get some necessary business of his own attended to while Portsmouth is in such a bustle. I hope Fanny has seen the Emperor, and then I may fairly wish them all away. I go to-morrow, and hope for some delays and adventures.

My mother's wood is brought in, but, by some mistake, no bavins. She must therefore buy some.

Henry at White's! Oh, what a Henry! I do not know what to wish as to Miss B., so I will hold my tongue and my wishes.

Sackree and the children set off yesterday, and have not been returned back upon us. They were all very well the evening before. We had handsome presents from the Gt. House yesterday,—a ham and the four leeches. Sackree has left some shirts of her master's at the school, which, finished or unfinished, she begs to have sent by Henry and Wm. Mr. Hinton is expected home soon, which is a good thing for the shirts.

We have called upon Miss Dusantoy and Miss Papillon, and been very pretty. Miss D. has a great idea of being Fanny Price,— she and her youngest sister together, who is named Fanny.

Miss Benn has drank tea with the Prowtings, and, I believe, comes to us this evening. She has still a swelling about the forefinger and a little discharge, and does not seem to be on the point of a perfect cure, but her spirits are good, and she will be most happy, I believe, to accept any invitation. The Clements are gone to Petersfield to look.

Only think of the Marquis of Granby being dead. I hope, if it please Heaven there should be another son, they will have better sponsors and less parade.

I certainly do not wish that Henry should think again of getting me to town. I would rather return straight from Bookham; but if he really does propose it, I cannot say No to what will be so kindly intended. It could be but for a few days, however, as my mother would be quite disappointed by my exceeding the fortnight which I now talk of as the outside—at least, we could not both remain longer away comfortably.

The middle of July is Martha's time, as far as she has any time. She has left it to Mrs. Craven to fix the day. I wish she could get her money paid, for I fear her going at all depends upon that.

Instead of Bath the Deans Dundases have taken a house at Clifton—Richmond Terrace—and she is as glad of the change as even you and I should be, or almost. She will now be able to go on from Berks and visit them without any fears from heat.

This post has brought me a letter from Miss Sharpe. Poor thing! she has been suffering indeed, but is now in a comparative state of comfort. She is at Sir W. P.'s, in Yorkshire, with the children, and there is no appearance of her quitting them. Of course we lose the pleasure of seeing her here. She writes highly of Sir Wm. I do so want him to marry her. There is a Dow. Lady P. presiding there to make it all right. The Man is the same; but she does not mention what he is by profession or trade. She does not think Lady P. was privy to his scheme on her, but, on being in his power, yielded. Oh, Sir Wm.! Sir Wm.! how I will love you if you will love Miss Sharpe!

Mrs. Driver, etc., are off by Collier, but so near being too late that she had not time to call and leave the keys herself. I have them, however. I suppose one is the key of the linen-press, but I do not know what to guess the other.

The coach was stopped at the blacksmith's, and they came running down with Triggs and Browning, and trunks, and birdcages. Quite amusing.

My mother desires her love, and hopes to hear from you.

Yours very affectionately,
J. AUSTEN.

Frank and Mary are to have Mary Goodchild to help as *Under* till they can get a cook. She is delighted to go.

Best love at Streatham.

Miss AUSTEN, Henrietta St.
By favor of Mr. GRAY.

LVII.

---

23 HANS PLACE, Tuesday morning (August, 1814).

MY DEAR CASSANDRA,—I had a very good journey, not crowded, two of the three taken up at Bentley being children, the others of a reasonable size; and they were all very quiet and civil. We were late in London, from being a great load, and from changing coaches at Farnham; it was nearly four, I believe, when we reached Sloane Street. Henry himself met me, and as soon as my trunk and basket could be routed out from all the other trunks and baskets in the world, we were on our way to Hans Place in the luxury of a nice, large, cool, dirty hackney coach.

There were four in the kitchen part of Yalden, and I was told fifteen at top, among them Percy Benn. We met in the same room at Egham, but poor Percy was not in his usual spirits. He would be more chatty, I dare say, in his way from Woolwich. We took up a young Gibson at Holybourn, and, in short, everybody either did come up by Yalden yesterday, or wanted to come up. It put me in mind of my own coach between Edinburgh and Stirling.

Henry is very well, and has given me an account of the Canterbury races, which seem to have been as pleasant as one could wish. Everything went well. Fanny had good partners, Mr. —— was her second on Thursday, but he did not dance with her any more.

This will content you for the present. I must just add, however, that there were no Lady Charlottes, they were gone off to Kirby, and that Mary Oxenden, instead of dying, is going to marry Wm. Hammond.

No James and Edward yet. Our evening yesterday was

perfectly quiet; we only talked a little to Mr. Tilson across the intermediate gardens; she was gone out airing with Miss Burdett. It is a delightful place,—more than answers my expectation. Having got rid of my unreasonable ideas, I find more space and comfort in the rooms than I had supposed, and the garden is quite a love. I am in the front attic, which is the bedchamber to be preferred.

Henry wants you to see it all, and asked whether you would return with him from Hampshire; I encouraged him to think you would. He breakfasts here early, and then rides to Henrietta St. If it continues fine, John is to drive me there by and by, and we shall take an airing together; and I do not mean to take any other exercise, for I feel a little tired after my long jumble. I live in his room downstairs; it is particularly pleasant from opening upon the garden. I go and refresh myself every now and then, and then come back to solitary coolness. There is one maidservant only, a very creditable, clean-looking young woman. Richard remains for the present.

Wednesday morning.—My brother and Edwd. arrived last night. They could not get places the day before. Their business is about teeth and wigs, and they are going after breakfast to Scarman's and Tavistock St., and they are to return to go with me afterwards in the barouche. I hope to do some of my errands to-day.

I got the willow yesterday, as Henry was not quite ready when I reached Hena. St. I saw Mr. Hampson there for a moment. He dines here to-morrow, and proposed bringing his son; so I must submit to seeing George Hampson, though I had hoped to go through life without it. It was one of my vanities, like your not reading "Patronage."

After leaving H. St. we drove to Mrs. Latouche's; they are always at home, and they are to dine here on Friday. We could do no more, as it began to rain.

We dine at half-past four to-day, that our visitors may go to the play, and Henry and I are to spend the evening with the

Tilsons, to meet Miss Burnett, who leaves town to-morrow. Mrs. T. called on me yesterday.

Is not this all that can have happened or been arranged? Not quite. Henry wants me to see more of his Hanwell favorite, and has written to invite her to spend a day or two here with me. His scheme is to fetch her on Saturday. I am more and more convinced that he will marry again soon, and like the idea of her better than of anybody else at hand.

Now I have breakfasted and have the room to myself again. It is likely to be a fine day. How do you all do?

Henry talks of being at Chawton about the 1st of Sept. He has once mentioned a scheme which I should rather like,—calling on the Birches and the Crutchleys in our way. It may never come to anything, but I must provide for the possibility by troubling you to send up my silk pelisse by Collier on Saturday. I feel it would be necessary on such an occasion; and be so good as to put up a clean dressing-gown which will come from the wash on Friday. You need not direct it to be left anywhere. It may take its chance.

We are to call for Henry between three and four, and I must finish this and carry it with me, as he is not always there in the morning before the parcel is made up. And before I set off, I must return Mrs. Tilson's visit. I hear nothing of the Hoblyns, and abstain from all inquiry.

I hope Mary Jane and Frank's gardens go on well. Give my love to them all—Nunna Hat's love to George. A great many people wanted to run up in the Poach as well as me. The wheat looked very well all the way, and James says the same of *his* road.

The same good account of Mrs. C.'s health continues, and her circumstances mend. She gets farther and farther from poverty. What a comfort! Good-by to you.

Yours very truly and affectionately,
JANE.

All well at Steventon. I hear nothing particular of Ben, except that Edward is to get him some pencils.

Miss AUSTEN, Chawton.
By favor of Mr. GRAY.

LVIII.

My dear Anna,[31]—I am very much obliged to you for sending your MS. It has entertained me extremely; indeed all of us. I read it aloud to your grandmamma and Aunt Cass, and we were all very much pleased. The spirit does not droop at all. Sir Thos., Lady Helen, and St. Julian are very well done, and Cecilia continues to be interesting in spite of her being so amiable. It was very fit you should advance her age. I like the beginning of Devereux Forester very much, a great deal better than if he had been very good or very bad. A few verbal corrections are all that I felt tempted to make; the principal of them is a speech of St. Julian to Lady Helen, which you see I have presumed to alter. As Lady H. is Cecilia's superior, it would not be correct to talk of her being introduced. It is Cecilia who must be introduced. And I do not like a lover speaking in the 3rd person; it is too much like the part of Lord Overtley, and I think it not natural. If you think differently, however, you need not mind me. I am impatient for more, and only wait for a safe conveyance to return this.

Yours affectionately,
J. A.

FOOTNOTE:

[31] Miss Anna Austen, at this time engaged to Mr. Lefroy, was writing a novel which she sent to her aunt for criticism.

LIX.

_____

AUGUST 10, 1814.

MY DEAR ANNA,—I am quite ashamed to find that I have never answered some question of yours in a former note. I kept it on purpose to refer to it at a proper time, and then forgot it. I like the name "Which is the Heroine" very well, and I dare say shall grow to like it very much in time; but "Enthusiasm" was something so very superior that my common title must appear to disadvantage. I am not sensible of any blunders about Dawlish; the library was pitiful and wretched twelve years ago, and not likely to have anybody's publications. There is no such title as Desborough, either among dukes, marquises, earls, viscounts, or barons. These were your inquiries. I will now thank you for your envelope received this morning. Your Aunt Cass is as well pleased with St. Julian as ever, and I am delighted with the idea of seeing Progillian again.

Wednesday, 17.—We have now just finished the first of the three books I had the pleasure of receiving yesterday. I read it aloud, and we are all very much amused, and like the work quite as well as ever. I depend on getting through another book before dinner, but there is really a good deal of respectable reading in your forty-eight pages. I have no doubt six would make a very good-sized volume. You must have been quite pleased to have accomplished so much. I like Lord Portman and his brother very much. I am only afraid that Lord P.'s good nature will make most people like him better than he deserves. The whole family are very good; and Lady Anne, who was your great dread, you have succeeded particularly well with. Bell Griffin is just what she should be. My corrections have not been more important than before; here and there we have thought the sense could be expressed in fewer words, and I have scratched out Sir Thos. from walking with the others to the stables, etc. the very day after breaking his arm; for though I find your papa did walk out immediately after his arm was set, I think it can be so little usual as to appear unnatural in a book. Lynn will not do. Lynn is towards forty miles from Dawlish and would not be talked of there. I have put Starcross instead. If you prefer Easton, that must be always safe.

I have also scratched out the introduction between Lord Portman and his brother and Mr. Griffin. A country surgeon (don't tell Mr. C. Lyford) would not be introduced to men of their rank; and when Mr. P. is first brought in, he would not be introduced as the Honorable. That distinction is never mentioned at such times; at least, I believe not. Now we have finished the second book, or rather the fifth. I do think you had better omit Lady Helena's postscript. To those that are acquainted with "Pride and Prejudice" it will seem an imitation. And your Aunt C. and I both recommend your making a little alteration in the last scene between Devereux F. and Lady Clanmurray and her daughter. We think they press him too much, more than sensible or well-bred women would do; Lady C., at least, should have discretion enough to be sooner satisfied with his determination of not going with them. I am very much pleased with Egerton as yet. I did not expect to like him, but I do, and Susan is a very nice little animated creature; but St. Julian is the delight of our lives. He is quite interesting. The whole of his break-off with Lady Helena is very well done. Yes; Russell Square is a very proper distance from Berkeley Square. We are reading the last book. They must be two days going from Dawlish to Bath. They are nearly one hundred miles apart.

Thursday.—We finished it last night after our return from drinking tea at the Great House. The last chapter does not please us quite so well; we do not thoroughly like the play, perhaps from having had too much of plays in that way lately (*vide* "Mansfield Park"), and we think you had better not leave England. Let the Portmans go to Ireland; but as you know nothing of the manners there, you had better not go with them. You will be in danger of giving false representations. Stick to Bath and the Foresters. There you will be quite at home.

Your Aunt C. does not like desultory novels, and is rather afraid yours will be too much so, that there will be too frequently a change from one set of people to another, and that circumstances will be introduced of apparent consequence which will lead to nothing. It will not be so great an objection to me if it does. I allow much more latitude than she does, and think Nature and spirit cover many sins of a wandering story, and people in general do not care so much about it for your comfort.

I should like to have had more of Devereux. I do not feel enough acquainted with him. You were afraid of meddling with him, I dare say. I like your sketch of Lord Clanmurray, and your picture of the two young girls' enjoyment is very good. I have not noticed St. Julian's serious conversation with Cecilia, but I like it exceedingly. What he says about the madness of otherwise sensible women on the subject of their daughters coming out is worth its weight in gold.

I do not perceive that the language sinks. Pray go on.

LX.

CHAWTON, Sept. 9.

MY DEAR ANNA,—We have been very much amused by your three books, but I have a good many criticisms to make, more than you will like. We are not satisfied with Mrs. Forester settling herself as tenant and near neighbor to such a man as Sir Thomas, without having some other inducement to go there. She ought to have some friend living thereabouts to tempt her. A woman going with two girls just growing up into a neighborhood where she knows nobody but one man of not very good character, is an awkwardness which so prudent a woman as Mrs. F. would not be likely to fall into. Remember she is very prudent. You must not let her act inconsistently. Give her a friend, and let that friend be invited by Sir Thomas H. to meet her, and we shall have no objection to her dining at the Priory as she does; but otherwise a woman in her situation would hardly go there before she had been visited by other families. I like the scene itself, the Miss Leslie, Lady Anne, and the music very much. Leslie is a noble name. Sir Thomas H. you always do very well. I have only taken the liberty of expunging one phrase of his which would not be allowable,—"Bless my heart!" It is too familiar and inelegant. Your grandmother is more disturbed at Mrs. Forester's not returning the Egertons' visit sooner than by anything else. They ought to have called at the Parsonage before Sunday. You describe a sweet place, but your descriptions are often more minute than will be liked. You give too many particulars of right hand and left. Mrs. Forester is not careful enough of Susan's health. Susan ought not to be walking out so soon after heavy rains, taking long walks in the dirt. An anxious mother would not suffer it. I like your Susan very much; she is a sweet creature, her playfulness of fancy is very delightful. I like her as she is now exceedingly, but I am not quite so well satisfied with her behavior to George R. At first she seems all over attachment and feeling, and afterwards to have none at all; she is so extremely confused at the ball, and so well satisfied apparently with Mr. Morgan. She seems to have changed her character.

You are now collecting your people delightfully, getting them exactly into such a spot as is the delight of my life. Three or four families in a country village is the very thing to work on, and I hope you will do a great deal more, and make full use of them while they are so very favorably arranged.

You are but now coming to the heart and beauty of your story. Until the heroine grows up the fun must be imperfect, but I expect a great deal of entertainment from the next three or four books, and I hope you will not resent these remarks by sending me no more. We like the Egertons very well. We see no blue pantaloons or cocks or hens. There is nothing to enchant one certainly in Mr. L. L., but we make no objection to him, and his inclination to like Susan is pleasing. The sister is a good contrast, but the name of Rachel is as much as I can bear. They are not so much like the Papillons as I expected. Your last chapter is very entertaining, the conversation on genius, etc.; Mr. St. Julian and Susan both talk in character, and very well. In some former parts Cecilia is perhaps a little too solemn and good, but upon the whole her disposition is very well opposed to Susan's, her want of imagination is very natural. I wish you could make Mrs. Forester talk more; but she must be difficult to manage and make entertaining, because there is so much good sense and propriety about her that nothing can be made very broad. Her economy and her ambition must not be staring. The papers left by Mrs. Fisher are very good. Of course one guesses something. I hope when you have written a great deal more, you will be equal to scratching out some of the past. The scene with Mrs. Mellish I should condemn; it is prosy and nothing to the purpose, and indeed the more you can find in your heart to curtail between Dawlish and Newton Priors, the better I think it will be,—one does not care for girls until they are grown up. Your Aunt C. quite understands the exquisiteness of that name,—Newton Priors is really a nonpareil. Milton would have given his eyes to have thought of it. Is not the cottage taken from Tollard Royal?

[Thus far the letter was written on the 9th, but before it was finished news arrived at Chawton of the death of Mrs. Charles Austen. She died in her confinement, and the baby died also. She left three little girls,—Cassie, Harriet, and Fanny. It was not until the 18th that Jane resumed her letter as follows:[32]]

Sunday.—I am very glad, dear Anna, that I wrote as I did before this sad event occurred. I have only to add that your grandmamma does not seem the worse now for the shock.

I shall be very happy to receive more of your work if more is ready; and you write so fast that I have great hopes Mr. Digweed will come back freighted with such a cargo as not all his hops or his sheep could equal the value of.

Your grandmamma desires me to say that she will have finished your shoes to-morrow, and thinks they will look very well. And that she depends upon seeing you, as you promise, before you quit the country, and hopes you will give her more than a day.

Yours affectionately.
J. AUSTEN.

FOOTNOTE:

[32] Note by Lord Brabourne.

LXI.

CHAWTON, Wednesday (Sept. 28).

MY DEAR ANNA,—I hope you do not depend on having your book again immediately. I kept it that your grandmamma may hear it, for it has not been possible yet to have any public reading. I have read it to your Aunt Cassandra, however, in our own room at night, while we undressed, and with a great deal of pleasure. We like the first chapter extremely, with only a little doubt whether Lady Helena is not almost too foolish. The matrimonial dialogue is very good certainly. I like Susan as well as ever, and begin now not to care at all about Cecilia; she may stay at Easton Court as long as she likes. Henry Mellish will be, I am afraid, too much in the common novel style,—a handsome, amiable, unexceptionable young man (such as do not much abound in real life), desperately in love and all in vain. But I have no business to judge him so early Jane Egerton is a very natural, comprehensible girl, and the whole of her acquaintance with Susan and Susan's letter to Cecilia are very pleasing and quite in character. But Miss Egerton does not entirely satisfy us. She is too formal and solemn, we think, in her advice to her brother not to fall in love; and it is hardly like a sensible woman,—it is putting it into his head. We should like a few hints from her better. We feel really obliged to you for introducing a Lady Kenrick; it will remove the greatest fault in the work, and I give you credit for considerable forbearance as an author in adopting so much of our opinion. I expect high fun about Mrs. Fisher and Sir Thomas. You have been perfectly right in telling Ben. Lefroy of your work, and I am very glad to hear how much he likes it. His encouragement and approbation must be "quite beyond everything."[33] I do not at all wonder at his not expecting to like anybody so well as Cecilia at first, but I shall be surprised if he does not become a Susanite in time. Devereux Forester's being ruined by his vanity is extremely good, but I wish you would not let him plunge into a "vortex of dissipation." I do not object to the thing, but I cannot bear the expression; it is such thorough novel slang, and so old that I dare say Adam met with it in the first novel he opened. Indeed, I did very much like to know Ben's opinion. I hope he will continue to be pleased with it, and I think he must, but I cannot flatter him with there being much incident. We have no great right to wonder at his not valuing the name of Progillian. That is a source of delight which even he can hardly be quite competent to.

Walter Scott has no business to write novels, especially good ones. It is not fair. He has fame and profit enough as a poet, and should not be taking the bread out of the mouths of other people.

I do not like him, and do not mean to like "Waverley" if I can help it, but fear I must.

I am quite determined, however, not to be pleased with Mrs. West's "Alicia De Lacy," should I ever meet with it, which I hope I shall not. I think I can be stout against anything written by Mrs. West. I have made up my mind to like no novels really but Miss Edgeworth's, yours, and my own.

What can you do with Egerton to increase the interest for him? I wish you could contrive something, some family occurrence to bring out his good qualities more. Some distress among brothers and sisters to relieve by the sale of his curacy! Something to carry him mysteriously away, and then be heard of at York or Edinburgh in an old greatcoat. I would not seriously recommend anything improbable, but if you could invent something spirited for him, it would have a good effect. He might lend all his money to Captain Morris, but then he would be a great fool if he did. Cannot the Morrises quarrel and he reconcile them? Excuse the liberty I take in these suggestions.

Your Aunt Frank's nursemaid has just given her warning, but

whether she is worth your having, or would take your place, I know not. She was Mrs. Webb's maid before she went to the Great House. She leaves your aunt because she cannot agree with the other servants. She is in love with the man, and her head seems rather turned. He returns her affection, but she fancies every one else is wanting him and envying her. Her previous service must have fitted her for such a place as yours, and she is very active and cleanly. The Webbs are really gone! When I saw the wagons at the door, and thought of all the trouble they must have in moving, I began to reproach myself for not having liked them better; but since the wagons have disappeared my conscience has been closed again, and I am excessively glad they are gone.

I am very fond of Sherlock's sermons, and prefer them to almost any.

Your affectionate aunt,
J. AUSTEN.

If you wish me to speak to the maid, let me know.

FOOTNOTE:

[33] A phrase always in the mouth of one of the Chawton neighbors, Mrs. H. Digweed.

LXII.

To Miss Frances Austen.

CHAWTON, Friday (Nov. 18, 1814).

I FEEL quite as doubtful as you could be, my dearest Fanny, as to when my letter may be finished, for I can command very little quiet time at present; but yet I must begin, for I know you will be glad to hear as soon as possible, and I really am impatient myself to be writing something on so very interesting a subject, though I have no hope of writing anything to the purpose. I shall do very little more, I dare say, than say over again what you have said before.

I was certainly a good deal surprised at first, as I had no suspicion of any change in your feelings, and I have no scruple in saying that you cannot be in love. My dear Fanny, I am ready to laugh at the idea, and yet it is no laughing matter to have had you so mistaken as to your own feelings. And with all my heart I wish I had cautioned you on that point when first you spoke to me; but though I did not think you then much in love, I did consider you as being attached in a degree quite sufficiently for happiness, as I had no doubt it would increase with opportunity, and from the time of our being in London together I thought you really very much in love. But you certainly are not at all—there is no concealing it.

What strange creatures we are! It seems as if your being secure of him had made you indifferent. There was a little disgust, I suspect, at the races, and I do not wonder at it. His expressions then would not do for one who had rather more acuteness, penetration, and taste, than love, which was your case. And yet, after all, I am surprised that the change in your feelings should be so great. He is just what he ever was, only more evidently and uniformly devoted to you. This is all the difference. How shall we account for it?

My dearest Fanny, I am writing what will not be of the smallest use to you. I am feeling differently every moment, and shall not be able to suggest a single thing that can assist your mind. I could lament in one sentence and laugh in the next, but as to opinion or counsel I am sure that none will be extracted worth having from this letter.

I read yours through the very evening I received it, getting away by myself. I could not bear to leave off when I had once begun. I was full of curiosity and concern. Luckily your At. C. dined at the other house; therefore I had not to man[oe]uvre away from her, and as to anybody else, I do not care.

Poor dear Mr. A.! Oh, dear Fanny! your mistake has been one that thousands of women fall into. He was the first young man who attached himself to you. That was the charm, and most powerful it is. Among the multitudes, however, that make the same mistake with yourself, there can be few indeed who have so little reason to regret it; his character and his attachment leave you nothing to be ashamed of.

Upon the whole, what is to be done? You have no inclination for any other person. His situation in life, family, friends, and, above all, his character, his uncommonly amiable mind, strict principles, just notions, good habits, all that you know so well how to value, all that is really of the first importance,—everything of this nature pleads his cause most strongly. You have no doubt of his having superior abilities, he has proved it at the University; he is, I dare say, such a scholar as your agreeable, idle brothers would ill bear a comparison with.

Oh, my dear Fanny! the more I write about him the warmer my feelings become,—the more strongly I feel the sterling worth of such a young man, and the desirableness of your growing in love with him again. I recommend this most thoroughly.

There are such beings in the world, perhaps one in a thousand, as the creature you and I should think perfection, where grace and spirit are united to worth, where the manners are equal to the heart and understanding; but such a person may not come in your way, or, if he does, he may not be the eldest son of a man of fortune, the near relation of your particular friend, and belonging to your own county.

Think of all this, Fanny. Mr. A. has advantages which we do not often meet in one person. His only fault, indeed, seems modesty. If he were less modest, he would be more agreeable, speak louder, and look impudenter; and is not it a fine character of which modesty is the only defect? I have no doubt he will get more lively and more like yourselves as he is more with you; he will catch your ways if he belongs to you. And as to there being any objection from his goodness, from the danger of his becoming even evangelical, I cannot admit that. I am by no means convinced that we ought not all to be evangelicals, and am at least persuaded that they who are so from reason and feeling must be happiest and safest. Do not be frightened from the connection by your brothers having most wit,—wisdom is better than wit, and in the long run will certainly have the laugh on her side; and don't be frightened by the idea of his acting more strictly up to the precepts of the New Testament than others.

And now, my dear Fanny, having written so much on one side of the question, I shall turn round and entreat you not to commit yourself farther, and not to think of accepting him unless you really do like him. Anything is to be preferred or endured rather than marrying without affection; and if his deficiencies of manner, etc., etc., strike you more than all his good qualities, if you continue to think strongly of them, give him up at once. Things are now in such a state that you must resolve upon one or the other,—either to allow him to go on as he has done, or whenever you are together behave with a coldness which may convince him that he has been deceiving himself. I have no doubt of his suffering a good deal for a time,—a great deal when he feels that he must give you up; but it is no creed of mine, as you must be well aware, that such sort of disappointments kill anybody.

Your sending the music was an admirable device, it made everything easy, and I do not know how I could have accounted for the parcel otherwise; for though your dear papa most conscientiously hunted about till he found me alone in the dining-parlor, your Aunt C. had seen that he had a parcel to deliver. As it was, however, I do not think anything was suspected.

We have heard nothing fresh from Anna. I trust she is very comfortable in her new home. Her letters have been very sensible and satisfactory, with no parade of happiness, which I liked them the better for. I have often known young married women write in a way I did not like in that respect.

You will be glad to hear that the first edition of M. P.[34] is all sold. Your Uncle Henry is rather wanting me to come to town to settle about a second edition; but as I could not very conveniently leave home now, I have written him my will and pleasure and unless he still urges it, shall not go. I am very greedy and want to make the most of it; but as you are much above caring about money, I shall not plague you with any particulars. The pleasures of vanity are more within your comprehension, and you will enter into mine at receiving the praise which every now and then comes to me through some channel or other.

Saturday.—Mr. Palmer spent yesterday with us, and is gone off with Cassy this morning. We have been expecting Miss Lloyd the last two days, and feel sure of her to-day. Mr. Knight and Mr. Edwd. Knight are to dine with us, and on Monday they are to dine with us again, accompanied by their respectable host and hostess.

Sunday.—Your papa had given me messages to you; but they are unnecessary, as he writes by this post to Aunt Louisa. We had a pleasant party yesterday; at least we found it so. It is delightful to see him so cheerful and confident. Aunt Cass. and I dine at the Great House to-day. We shall be a snug half-dozen. Miss Lloyd came, as we expected, yesterday, and desires her love. She is very happy to hear of your learning the harp. I do not mean to send you what I owe Miss Hare, because I think you would rather not be paid beforehand.

Yours very affectionately,
JANE AUSTEN.

Miss KNIGHT,
Goodnestone Farm, Wingham, Kent.

FOOTNOTE:

[34] "Mansfield Park."

LXIII.

—————————————

CHAWTON, Nov. 21, 1814.

MY DEAR ANNA,—I met Harriet Benn yesterday. She gave me her congratulations, and desired they might be forwarded to you, and there they are. The chief news from this country is the death of old Mrs. Dormer. Mrs. Clement walks about in a new black velvet pelisse lined with yellow, and a white bobbin net veil, and looks remarkably well in them.

I think I understand the country about Hendon from your description. It must be very pretty in summer. Should you know from the atmosphere that you were within a dozen miles of London? Make everybody at Hendon admire "Mansfield Park."

Your affectionate aunt,
J. A.

LXIV.

HANS PLACE, Nov. 28, 1814.

MY DEAR ANNA,—I assure you we all came away very much pleased with our visit. We talked of you for about a mile and a half with great satisfaction; and I have been just sending a very good report of you to Miss Benn, with a full account of your dress for Susan and Maria.

We were all at the play last night to see Miss O'Neil in "Isabella." I do not think she was quite equal to my expectations. I fancy I want something more than can be. I took two pocket-handkerchiefs, but had very little occasion for either. She is an elegant creature, however, and hugs Mr. Young delightfully. I am going this morning to see the little girls in Keppel Street. Cassy was excessively interested about your marriage when she heard of it, which was not until she was to drink your health on the wedding-day.

She asked a thousand questions in her usual manner, what he said to you and what you said to him. If your uncle were at home he would send his best love, but I will not impose any base fictitious remembrances on you; mine I can honestly give, and remain

Your affectionate aunt,
J. AUSTEN.

LXV.

HANS PLACE, Wednesday.

MY DEAR ANNA,—I have been very far from finding your book an evil, I assure you. I read it immediately and with great pleasure. I think you are going on very well. The description of Dr. Griffin and Lady Helena's unhappiness is very good, and just what was likely to be. I am curious to know what the end of them will be. The name of Newton Priors is really invaluable; I never met with anything superior to it. It is delightful, and one could live on the name of Newton Priors for a twelvemonth. Indeed, I think you get on very fast. I only wish other people of my acquaintance could compose as rapidly. I am pleased with the dog scene and with the whole of George and Susan's love, but am more particularly struck with your serious conversations. They are very good throughout. St. Julian's history was quite a surprise to me. You had not very long known it yourself, I suspect; but I have no objection to make to the circumstance, and it is very well told. His having been in love with the aunt gives Cecilia an additional interest with him. I like the idea,—a very proper compliment to an aunt! I rather imagine indeed that nieces are seldom chosen but out of compliment to some aunt or another. I dare say Ben was in love with me once, and would never have thought of you if he had not supposed me dead of scarlet fever. Yes, I was in a mistake as to the number of books. I thought I had read three before the three at Chawton, but fewer than six will not do. I want to see dear Bell Griffin again; and had you not better give some hint of St. Julian's early history in the beginning of the story?

We shall see nothing of Streatham while we are in town, as Mrs. Hill is to lie in of a daughter. Mrs. Blackstone is to be with her. Mrs. Heathcote and Miss Bigg[35] are just leaving. The latter writes me word that Miss Blackford is married, but I have never seen it in the papers, and one may as well be single if the wedding is not to be in print.

Your affectionate aunt,
J. A.

LXVI.

23 HANS PLACE, Wednesday (Nov. 30, 1814).

I AM very much obliged to you, my dear Fanny, for your letter, and I hope you will write again soon, that I may know you to be all safe and happy at home.

Our visit to Hendon will interest you, I am sure; but I need not enter into the particulars of it, as your papa will be able to answer almost every question. I certainly could describe her bedroom and her drawers and her closet better than he can, but I do not feel that I can stop to do it. I was rather sorry to hear that she is to have an instrument; it seems throwing money away. They will wish the twenty-four guineas in the shape of sheets and towels six months hence; and as to her playing, it never can be anything.

Her purple pelisse rather surprised me. I thought we had known all paraphernalia of that sort. I do not mean to blame her; it looked very well, and I dare say she wanted it. I suspect nothing worse than its being got in secret, and not owned to anybody. I received a very kind note from her yesterday, to ask me to come again and stay a night with them. I cannot do it, but I was pleased to find that she had the power of doing so right a thing. My going was to give them both pleasure very properly.

I just saw Mr. Hayter at the play, and think his face would please me on acquaintance. I was sorry he did not dine here. It seemed rather odd to me to be in the theatre with nobody to watch for. I was quite composed myself, at leisure for all the agitated Isabella could raise.

Now, my dearest Fanny, I will begin a subject which comes in very naturally. You frighten me out of my wits by your reference.

Your affection gives me the highest pleasure, but indeed you must not let anything depend on my opinion; your own feelings, and none but your own, should determine such an important point. So far, however, as answering your question, I have no scruple. I am perfectly convinced that your present feelings, supposing that you were to marry now, would be sufficient for his happiness; but when I think how very, very far it is from a "now," and take everything that may be into consideration, I dare not say, "Determine to accept him;" the risk is too great for you, unless your own sentiments prompt it.

You will think me perverse, perhaps; in my last letter I was urging everything in his favor, and now I am inclining the other way, but I cannot help it; I am at present more impressed with the possible evil that may arise to you from engaging yourself to him—in word or mind—than with anything else. When I consider how few young men you have yet seen much of, how capable you are (yes, I do still think you very capable) of being really in love, and how full of temptation the next six or seven years of your life will probably be (it is the very period of life for the strongest attachments to be formed),—I cannot wish you, with your present very cool feelings, to devote yourself in honor to him. It is very true that you never may attach another man his equal altogether; but if that other man has the power of attaching you more, he will be in your eyes the most perfect.

I shall be glad if you can revive past feelings, and from your unbiassed self resolve to go on as you have done, but this I do not expect; and without it I cannot wish you to be fettered. I should not be afraid of your marrying him; with all his worth you would soon love him enough for the happiness of both; but I should dread the continuance of this sort of tacit engagement, with such an uncertainty as there is of when it may be completed. Years may pass before he is independent; you like him well enough to marry, but not well enough to wait; the unpleasantness of appearing fickle is certainly great; but if you think you want punishment for past illusions, there it is, and nothing can be compared to the misery of being bound without love,—bound to one, and preferring another; that is a punishment which you do not deserve.

I know you did not meet, or rather will not meet, to-day, as he called here yesterday; and I am glad of it. It does not seem very likely, at least, that he should be in time for a dinner visit sixty miles off. We did not see him, only found his card when we came home at four. Your Uncle H. merely observed that he was a day after "the fair." We asked your brother on Monday (when Mr. Hayter was talked of) why he did not invite him too; saying, "I know he is in town, for I met him the other day in Bond St." Edward answered that he did not know where he was to be found. "Don't you know his chambers?" "No."

I shall be most glad to hear from you again, my dearest Fanny, but it must not be later than Saturday, as we shall be off on Monday long before the letters are delivered; and write something that may do to be read or told. I am to take the Miss Moores back on Saturday, and when I return I shall hope to find your pleasant little flowing scrawl on the table. It will be a relief to me after playing at ma'ams, for though I like Miss H. M. as much as one can at my time of life after a day's acquaintance, it is uphill work to be talking to those whom one knows so little.

Only one comes back with me to-morrow, probably Miss Eliza, and I rather dread it. We shall not have two ideas in common. She is young, pretty, chattering, and thinking chiefly, I presume, of dress, company, and admiration. Mr. Sanford is to join us at dinner, which will be a comfort, and in the evening, while your uncle and Miss Eliza play chess, he shall tell me comical things and I will laugh at them, which will be a pleasure to both.

I called in Keppel Street and saw them all, including dear Uncle Charles, who is to come and dine with us quietly to-day. Little Harriot sat in my lap, and seemed as gentle and affectionate as ever, and as pretty, except not being quite well. Fanny is a fine stout girl, talking incessantly, with an interesting degree of lisp and indistinctness, and very likely may be the handsomest in time. Cassy did not show more pleasure in seeing me than her sisters, but I expected no better. She does not shine in the tender feelings. She will never be a Miss O'Neil, more in the Mrs. Siddons line.

Thank you, but it is not settled yet whether I do hazard a second edition. We are to see Egerton to-day, when it will probably be determined. People are more ready to borrow and praise than to buy, which I cannot wonder at; but though I like praise as well as anybody, I like what Edward calls "Pewter" too. I hope he continues careful of his eyes, and finds the good effect of it. I cannot suppose we differ in our ideas of the Christian religion. You have given an excellent description of it. We only affix a different meaning to the word *evangelical*.

Yours most affectionately,
J. AUSTEN.

Miss KNIGHT,
Godmersham Park, Faversham, Kent.

FOOTNOTE:

[35] Sisters to Mrs. Hall.

LXVII.

CHAWTON, Friday (Sept. 29).

MY DEAR ANNA,—We told Mr. B. Lefroy that if the weather did not prevent us we should certainly come and see you to-morrow and bring Cassy, trusting to your being good enough to give her a dinner about one o'clock, that we might be able to be with you the earlier and stay the longer. But on giving Cassy her choice between the Fair at Alton or Wyards, it must be confessed that she has preferred the former, which we trust will not greatly affront you; if it does, you may hope that some little Anne hereafter may revenge the insult by a similar preference of an Alton Fair to her Cousin Cassy. In the mean while we have determined to put off our visit to you until Monday, which we hope will be not less convenient. I wish the weather may not resolve on another put off. I must come to you before Wednesday if it be possible, for on that day I am going to London for a week or two with your Uncle Henry, who is expected here on Sunday. If Monday should appear too dirty for walking, and Mr. Lefroy would be so kind as to come and fetch me, I should be much obliged to him. Cassy might be of the party, and your Aunt Cassandra will take another opportunity.

Yours very affectionately, my dear Anna,
J. AUSTEN.

Note by Lord Brabourne.
But before the week or two to which she had limited her visit in Hans Place was at an end, her brother fell ill, and on October 22

he was in such danger that she wrote to Steventon to summon her father to town. The letter was two days on the road, and reached him on Sunday the 24th. Even then he did not start immediately. In the evening he and his wife rode to Chawton, and it was not until the next day that he and Cassandra arrived in Hans Place. The malady from which Henry Austen was suffering was low fever, and he was for some days at death's door: but he rallied soon after his brother and sisters arrived, and recovered so quickly that the former was able to leave him at the end of the week. The great anxiety and fatigue which Jane underwent at this time was supposed by some of her family to have broken down her health. She was in a very feeble and exhausted condition when the bank in which her brother Henry was a partner broke, and he not only lost all that he possessed, but most of his relations suffered severely also. Jane was well enough to pay several visits with her sister in the summer of 1816, including one to Steventon,—the last she ever paid to that home of her childhood. The last note which Mrs. Lefroy had preserved is dated,—

LXVIII.

JUNE 23, 1816.

MY DEAR ANNA,—Cassy desires her best thanks for the book. She was quite delighted to see it. I do not know when I have seen her so much struck by anybody's kindness as on this occasion. Her sensibility seems to be opening to the perception of great actions. These gloves having appeared on the pianoforte ever since you were here on Friday, we imagine they must be yours. Mrs. Digweed returned yesterday through all the afternoon's rain, and was of course wet through; but in speaking of it she never once said "it was beyond everything," which I am sure it must have been. Your mamma means to ride to Speen Hill to-morrow to see the Mrs. Hulberts, who are both very indifferent. By all accounts they really are breaking now,—not so stout as the old jackass.

Yours affectionately,
J. A.

CHAWTON, Sunday, June 23.
Uncle Charles's birthday.

LXIX.

HANS PLACE, Friday (Nov. 24, 1815).

MY DEAREST CASSANDRA,—I have the pleasure of sending you a much better account of my affairs, which I know will be a great delight to you.

I wrote to Mr. Murray yesterday myself, and Henry wrote at the same time to Roworth. Before the notes were out of the house, I received three sheets and an apology from R. We sent the notes, however, and I had a most civil one in reply from Mr. M. He is so very polite, indeed, that it is quite overcoming. The printers have been waiting for paper,—the blame is thrown upon the stationer; but he gives his word that I shall have no further cause for dissatisfaction. He has lent us Miss Williams and Scott, and says that any book of his will always be at my service. In short, I am soothed and complimented into tolerable comfort.

We had a visit yesterday from Edwd. Knight, and Mr. Mascall joined him here; and this morning has brought Mr. Mascall's compliments and two pheasants. We have some hope of Edward's coming to dinner to-day; he will, if he can, I believe. He is looking extremely well.

To-morrow Mr. Haden is to dine with us. There is happiness! We really grow so fond of Mr. Haden that I do not know what to expect. He and Mr. Tilson and Mr. Philips made up our circle of wits last night. Fanny played, and he sat and listened and suggested improvements, till Richard came in to tell him that "the doctor was waiting for him at Captn. Blake's;" and then he was off with a speed that you can imagine. He never does appear in the least above his profession or out of humor with it, or I should think poor Captn. Blake, whoever he is, in a very bad way.

I must have misunderstood Henry when I told you that you were to hear from him to-day. He read me what he wrote to Edward: part of it must have amused him, I am sure one part, alas! cannot be very amusing to anybody. I wonder that with such business to worry him he can be getting better; but he certainly does gain strength, and if you and Edwd. were to see him now, I feel sure that you would think him improved since Monday.

He was out yesterday; it was a fine sunshiny day here (in the country perhaps you might have clouds and fogs. Dare I say so? I shall not deceive you, if I do, as to my estimation of the climate of London), and he ventured first on the balcony and then as far as the greenhouse. He caught no cold, and therefore has done more to-day, with great delight and self-persuasion of improvement.

He has been to see Mrs. Tilson and the Malings. By the by, you may talk to Mr. T. of his wife's being better; I saw her yesterday, and was sensible of her having gained ground in the last two days.

Evening.—We have had no Edward. Our circle is formed,— only Mr. Tilson and Mr. Haden. We are not so happy as we were. A message came this afternoon from Mrs. Latouche and Miss East, offering themselves to drink tea with us to-morrow, and, as it was accepted, here is an end of our extreme felicity in our dinner guest. I am heartily sorry they are coming; it will be an evening spoilt to Fanny and me.

Another little disappointment: Mr. H. advises Henry's not venturing with us in the carriage to-morrow; if it were spring, he says, it would be a different thing. One would rather this had not been. He seems to think his going out to-day rather imprudent, though acknowledging at the same time that he is better than he was in the morning.

Fanny has had a letter full of commissions from Goodnestone; we shall be busy about them and her own matters, I dare say, from twelve to four. Nothing, I trust, will keep us from Keppel Street.

This day has brought a most friendly letter from Mr. Fowle, with a brace of pheasants. I did not know before that Henry had written to him a few days ago to ask for them. We shall live upon pheasants,—no bad life!

I send you five one-pound notes, for fear you should be distressed for little money. Lizzy's work is charmingly done; shall you put it to your chintz? A sheet came in this moment; 1st and 3rd vols. are now at 144; 2nd at 48. I am sure you will like particulars. We are not to have the trouble of returning the sheets to Mr. Murray any longer; the printer's boys bring and carry.

I hope Mary continues to get well fast, and I send my love to little Herbert. You will tell me more of Martha's plans, of course, when you write again. Remember me most kindly to everybody, and Miss Benn besides.

Yours very affectionately,
J. AUSTEN.

I have been listening to dreadful insanity. It is Mr. Haden's firm belief that a person not musical is fit for every sort of wickedness. I ventured to assert a little on the other side, but wished the cause in abler hands.

Miss AUSTEN, Chawton.

LXX.

HANS PLACE, Sunday (Nov. 26).

MY DEAREST,—The parcel arrived safely, and I am much obliged to you for your trouble. It cost 2s. 10d., but as there is a certain saving of 2s. 4½d. on the other side, I am sure it is well worth doing. I send four pair of silk stockings, but I do not want them washed at present. In the three neckhandkerchiefs I include the one sent down before. These things, perhaps, Edwd. may be able to bring, but even if he is not, I am extremely pleased with his returning to you from Steventon. It is much better, far preferable.

I did mention the P. R. in my note to Mr. Murray; it brought me a fine compliment in return. Whether it has done any other good I do not know, but Henry thought it worth trying.

The printers continue to supply me very well. I am advanced in Vol. III. to my *arra*-root, upon which peculiar style of spelling there is a modest query in the margin. I will not forget Anna's arrowroot. I hope you have told Martha of my first resolution of letting nobody know that I might dedicate, etc., for fear of being obliged to do it, and that she is thoroughly convinced of my being influenced now by nothing but the most mercenary motives. I have paid nine shillings on her account to Miss Palmer; there was no more owing.

Well, we were very busy all yesterday; from half-past eleven till four in the streets, working almost entirely for other people, driving from place to place after a parcel for Sandling, which we could never find, and encountering the miseries of Grafton House to get a purple frock for Eleanor Bridges. We got to Keppel St., however, which was all I cared for; and though we could stay only a quarter of an hour, Fanny's calling gave great pleasure, and her sensibility still greater, for she was very much affected at the sight of the children. Poor little F. looked heavy. We saw the whole party.

Aunt Harriet hopes Cassy will not forget to make a pincushion for Mrs. Kelly, as she has spoken of its being promised her several times. I hope we shall see Aunt H. and the dear little girls here on Thursday.

So much for the morning. Then came the dinner and Mr. Haden, who brought good manners and clever conversation. From seven to eight the harp; at eight Mrs. L. and Miss E. arrived, and for the rest of the evening the drawing-room was thus arranged: on the sofa side the two ladies, Henry, and myself making the best of it; on the opposite side Fanny and Mr. Haden, in two chairs (I believe, at least, they had two chairs), talking together uninterruptedly. Fancy the scene! And what is to be fancied next? Why, that Mr. H. dines here again to-morrow. To-day we are to have Mr. Barlow. Mr. H. is reading "Mansfield Park" for the first time, and prefers it to P. and P.

A hare and four rabbits from Gm. yesterday, so that we are stocked for nearly a week. Poor Farmer Andrews! I am very sorry for him, and sincerely wish his recovery.

A better account of the sugar than I could have expected. I should like to help you break some more. I am glad you cannot wake early; I am sure you must have been under great arrears of rest.

Fanny and I have been to B. Chapel, and walked back with Maria Cuthbert. We have been very little plagued with visitors this last week. I remember only Miss Herries, the aunt, but I am in terror for to-day, a fine bright Sunday; plenty of mortar, and nothing to do.

Henry gets out in his garden every day, but at present his inclination for doing more seems over, nor has he now any plan for leaving London before Dec. 18, when he thinks of going to Oxford for a few days; to-day, indeed, his feelings are for continuing where he is through the next two months.

One knows the uncertainty of all this; but should it be so, we must think the best, and hope the best, and do the best; and my idea in that case is, that when he goes to Oxford I should go home, and have nearly a week of you before you take my place. This is only a silent project, you know, to be gladly given up if better things occur. Henry calls himself stronger every day, and Mr. H. keeps on approving his pulse, which seems generally better than ever, but still they will not let him be well. Perhaps when Fanny is gone he will be allowed to recover faster.

I am not disappointed: I never thought the little girl at Wyards very pretty, but she will have a fine complexion and curly hair, and pass for a beauty. We are glad the mamma's cold has not been worse, and send her our love and good wishes by every convenient opportunity. Sweet, amiable Frank! why does he have a cold too? Like Captain Mirvan to Mr. Duval,[36] "I wish it well over with him."

Fanny has heard all that I have said to you about herself and Mr. H. Thank you very much for the sight of dearest Charles's letter to yourself. How pleasantly and how naturally he writes! and how perfect a picture of his disposition and feelings his style conveys! Poor dear fellow! Not a present!

I have a great mind to send him all the twelve copies which were to have been dispersed among my near connections, beginning with the P. R.[37] and ending with Countess Morley. Adieu.

Yours affectionately,
J. AUSTEN.

Give my love to Cassy and Mary Jane. Caroline will be gone when this reaches you.

Miss AUSTEN.

FOOTNOTES:

[36] Characters in Miss Burney's "Evelina."
[37] Prince Regent.

LXXI.

HANS PLACE, Saturday (Dec. 2).

MY DEAR CASSANDRA,—Henry came back yesterday, and might have returned the day before if he had known as much in time. I had the pleasure of hearing from Mr. T. on Wednesday night that Mr. Seymour thought there was not the least occasion for his absenting himself any longer.

I had also the comfort of a few lines on Wednesday morning from Henry himself, just after your letter was gone, giving so good an account of his feelings as made me perfectly easy. He met with the utmost care and attention at Hanwell, spent his two days there very quietly and pleasantly, and being certainly in no respect the worse for going, we may believe that he must be better, as he is quite sure of being himself. To make his return a complete gala, Mr. Haden was secured for dinner. I need not say that our evening was agreeable.

But you seem to be under a mistake as to Mr. H. You call him an apothecary. He is no apothecary; he has never been an apothecary; there is not an apothecary in this neighborhood,— the only inconvenience of the situation, perhaps,—but so it is; we have not a medical man within reach. He is a Haden, nothing but a Haden, a sort of wonderful nondescript creature on two legs, something between a man and an angel, but without the least spice of an apothecary. He is, perhaps, the only person not an apothecary hereabouts. He has never sung to us. He will not sing without a pianoforte accompaniment.

Mr. Meyers gives his three lessons a week, altering his days and his hours, however, just as he chooses, never very punctual,

251

and never giving good measure. I have not Fanny's fondness for masters, and Mr. Meyers does not give me any longing after them. The truth is, I think, that they are all, at least music-masters, made of too much consequence, and allowed to take too many liberties with their scholars' time.

We shall be delighted to see Edward on Monday, only sorry that you must be losing him. A turkey will be equally welcome with himself. He must prepare for his own proper bedchamber here, as Henry moved down to the one below last week; he found the other cold.

I am sorry my mother has been suffering, and am afraid this exquisite weather is too good to agree with her. I enjoy it all over me, from top to toe, from right to left, longitudinally, perpendicularly, diagonally; and I cannot but selfishly hope we are to have it last till Christmas,—nice, unwholesome, unseasonable, relaxing, close, muggy weather.

Oh, thank you very much for your long letter; it did me a great deal of good. Henry accepts your offer of making his nine gallon of mead thankfully. The mistake of the dogs rather vexed him for a moment, but he has not thought of it since. To-day he makes a third attempt at his strengthening plaister, and as I am sure he will now be getting out a great deal, it is to be wished that he may be able to keep it on. He sets off this morning by the Chelsea coach to sign bonds and visit Henrietta St., and I have no doubt will be going every day to Henrietta St.

Fanny and I were very snug by ourselves as soon as we were satisfied about our invalid's being safe at Hanwell. By man[oe]uvring and good luck we foiled all the Malings' attempts upon us. Happily I caught a little cold on Wednesday, the morning we were in town, which we made very useful, and we saw nobody but our precious[38] and Mr. Tilson.

This evening the Malings are allowed to drink tea with us. We are in hopes—that is, we wish—Miss Palmer and the little girls may come this morning. You know, of course, that she could not come on Thursday, and she will not attempt to name any other day.

God bless you. Excuse the shortness of this, but I must finish it now, that I may save you 2*d*. Best love.

Yours affectionately,

J. A.

It strikes me that I have no business to give the P. R. a binding, but we will take counsel upon the question.

I am glad you have put the flounce on your chintz; I am sure it must look particularly well, and it is what I had thought of.

Miss AUSTEN,
Chawton, Alton, Hants.

FOOTNOTE:

[38] Probably a playful allusion to Mr. Haden.

LXXII.

CHAWTON (Feb. 20, 1816).

MY DEAREST FANNY,—You are inimitable, irresistible. You are the delight of my life. Such letters, such entertaining letters, as you have lately sent! such a description of your queer little heart! such a lovely display of what imagination does! You are worth your weight in gold, or even in the new silver coinage. I cannot express to you what I have felt in reading your history of yourself,—how full of pity and concern, and admiration and amusement I have been! You are the paragon of all that is silly and sensible, commonplace and eccentric, sad and lively, provoking and interesting. Who can keep pace with the fluctuations of your fancy, the capprizios of your taste, the contradictions of your feelings? You are so odd, and all the time so perfectly natural!—so peculiar in yourself, and yet so like everybody else!

It is very, very gratifying to me to know you so intimately. You can hardly think what a pleasure it is to me to have such thorough pictures of your heart. Oh, what a loss it will be when you are married! You are too agreeable in your single state,—too agreeable as a niece. I shall hate you when your delicious play of mind is all settled down into conjugal and maternal affections.

Mr. B—— frightens me. He will have you. I see you at the altar. I have some faith in Mrs. C. Cage's observation, and still more in Lizzy's; and besides, I know it must be so. He must be wishing to attach you. It would be too stupid and too shameful in him to be otherwise; and all the family are seeking your acquaintance.

Do not imagine that I have any real objection; I have rather taken a fancy to him than not, and I like the house for you. I only do not like you should marry anybody. And yet I do wish you to marry very much, because I know you will never be happy till you are; but the loss of a Fanny Knight will be never made up to me. My "affec. niece F. C. B——" will be but a poor substitute. I do not like your being nervous, and so apt to cry,—it is a sign you are not quite well; but I hope Mr. Scud—as you always write his name (your Mr. Scuds amuse me very much)—will do you good.

What a comfort that Cassandra should be so recovered! It was more than we had expected. I can easily believe she was very patient and very good. I always loved Cassandra for her fine dark eyes and sweet temper. I am almost entirely cured of my rheumatism,—just a little pain in my knee now and then, to make me remember what it was, and keep on flannel. Aunt Cassandra nursed me so beautifully.

I enjoy your visit to Goodnestone, it must be a great pleasure to you; you have not seen Fanny Cage in comfort so long. I hope she represents and remonstrates and reasons with you properly. Why should you be living in dread of his marrying somebody else? (Yet how natural!) You did not choose to have him yourself, why not allow him to take comfort where he can? In your conscience you know that he could not bear a companion with a more animated character. You cannot forget how you felt under the idea of its having been possible that he might have dined in Hans Place.

My dearest Fanny, I cannot bear you should be unhappy about him. Think of his principles; think of his father's objection, of want of money, etc., etc. But I am doing no good; no, all that I urge against him will rather make you take his part more,— sweet, perverse Fanny.

And now I will tell you that we like your Henry to the utmost, to the very top of the glass, quite brimful. He is a very pleasing young man. I do not see how he could be mended. He does really bid fair to be everything his father and sister could wish; and William I love very much indeed, and so we do all; he is quite our own William. In short, we are very comfortable together; that is, we can answer for ourselves.

Mrs. Deedes is as welcome as May to all our benevolence to her son; we only lamented that we could not do more, and that the 50*l.* note we slipped into his hand at parting was necessarily the limit of our offering. Good Mrs. Deedes! Scandal and gossip; yes, I dare say you are well stocked, but I am very fond of Mrs. —— for reasons good. Thank you for mentioning her praise of "Emma," etc.

I have contributed the marking to Uncle H.'s shirts, and now they are a complete memorial of the tender regard of many.

Friday.—I had no idea when I began this yesterday of sending it before your brother went back, but I have written away my foolish thoughts at such a rate that I will not keep them many hours longer to stare me in the face.

Much obliged for the quadrilles, which I am grown to think pretty enough, though of course they are very inferior to the cotillons of my own day.

Ben and Anna walked here last Sunday to hear Uncle Henry, and she looked so pretty, it was quite a pleasure to see her, so young and so blooming and so innocent, as if she had never had a wicked thought in her life, which yet one has some reason to suppose she must have had, if we believe the doctrine of original sin. I hope Lizzy will have her play very kindly arranged for her. Henry is generally thought very good-looking, but not so handsome as Edward. I think I prefer his face. Wm. is in excellent looks, has a fine appetite, and seems perfectly well. You will have a great break up at Godmersham in the spring. You must feel their all going. It is very right, however! Poor Miss C.! I shall pity her when she begins to understand herself.

Your objection to the quadrilles delighted me exceedingly. Pretty well, for a lady irrecoverably attached to one person! Sweet Fanny, believe no such thing of yourself, spread no such malicious slander upon your understanding within the precincts of your imagination. Do not speak ill of your sense merely for the gratification of your fancy; yours is sense which deserves more honorable treatment. You are not in love with him; you never have been really in love with him.

Yours very affectionately,
J. AUSTEN.

Miss KNIGHT,
Godmersham Park, Faversham, Kent.

LXXIII.

CHAWTON, Thursday (March 13).

As to making any adequate return for such a letter as yours, my dearest Fanny, it is absolutely impossible. If I were to labor at it all the rest of my life, and live to the age of Methuselah, I could never accomplish anything so long and so perfect; but I cannot let William go without a few lines of acknowledgment and reply.

I have pretty well done with Mr. ——. By your description, he cannot be in love with you, however he may try at it; and I could not wish the match unless there were a great deal of love on his side. I do not know what to do about Jemima Branfill. What does her dancing away with so much spirit mean? That she does not care for him, or only wishes to appear not to care for him? Who can understand a young lady?

Poor Mrs. C. Milles, that she should die on the wrong day at last, after being about it so long! It was unlucky that the Goodnestone party could not meet you; and I hope her friendly, obliging, social spirit, which delighted in drawing people together, was not conscious of the division and disappointment she was occasioning. I am sorry and surprised that you speak of her as having little to leave, and must feel for Miss Milles, though she is Molly, if a material loss of income is to attend her other loss. Single women have a dreadful propensity for being poor, which is one very strong argument in favor of matrimony; but I need not dwell on such arguments with you, pretty dear.

To you I shall say, as I have often said before, Do not be in a hurry, the right man will come at last; you will in the course of the next two or three years meet with somebody more generally unexceptionable than any one you have yet known, who will love you as warmly as possible, and who will so completely attract you that you will feel you never really loved before.

Do none of the A.'s ever come to balls now? You have never mentioned them as being at any. And what do you hear of the Gripps, or of Fanny and her husband?

Aunt Cassandra walked to Wyards yesterday with Mrs. Digweed. Anna has had a bad cold, and looks pale. She has just weaned Julia.

I have also heard lately from your Aunt Harriot, and cannot understand their plans in parting with Miss S., whom she seems very much to value now that Harriot and Eleanor are both of an age for a governess to be so useful to, especially as, when Caroline was sent to school some years, Miss Bell was still retained, though the others even then were nursery children. They have some good reason, I dare say, though I cannot penetrate it; and till I know what it is I shall invent a bad one, and amuse myself with accounting for the difference of measures by supposing Miss S. to be a superior sort of woman, who has never stooped to recommend herself to the master of the family by flattery, as Miss Bell did.

I will answer your kind questions more than you expect. "Miss Catherine" is put upon the shelf for the present, and I do not know that she will ever come out; but I have a something ready for publication, which may, perhaps, appear about a twelvemonth hence. It is short,—about the length of "Catherine." This is for yourself alone. Neither Mr. Salusbury nor Mr. Wildman is to know of it.

I am got tolerably well again, quite equal to walking about and enjoying the air, and by sitting down and resting a good while between my walks I get exercise enough. I have a scheme, however, for accomplishing more, as the weather grows spring-like. I mean to take to riding the donkey; it will be more independent and less troublesome than the use of the carriage, and I shall be able to go about with Aunt Cassandra in her walks to Alton and Wyards.

I hope you will think Wm. looking well; he was bilious the other day, and At. Cass. supplied him with a dose at his own request. I am sure you would have approved it. Wm. and I are the best of friends. I love him very much. Everything is so natural about him,—his affections, his manners, and his drollery. He entertains and interests us extremely.

Mat. Hammond and A. M. Shaw are people whom I cannot care for in themselves, but I enter into their situation, and am glad they are so happy. If I were the Duchess of Richmond, I should be very miserable about my son's choice.

Our fears increase for poor little Harriot; the latest account is that Sir Ev. Home is confirmed in his opinion of there being water on the brain. I hope Heaven, in its mercy, will take her soon. Her poor father will be quite worn out by his feelings for her; he cannot spare Cassy at present, she is an occupation and a comfort to him.

LXXIV.

CHAWTON, Sunday (March 23).

I AM very much obliged to you, my dearest Fanny, for sending me Mr. W.'s conversation; I had great amusement in reading it, and I hope I am not affronted, and do not think the worse of him for having a brain so very different from mine; but my strongest sensation of all is astonishment at your being able to press him on the subject so perseveringly; and I agree with your papa that it was not fair. When he knows the truth, he will be uncomfortable.

You are the oddest creature! Nervous enough in some respects, but in others perfectly without nerves! Quite unrepulsable, hardened, and impudent. Do not oblige him to read any more. Have mercy on him, tell him the truth, and make him an apology. He and I should not in the least agree, of course, in our ideas of novels and heroines. Pictures of perfection, as you know, make me sick and wicked; but there is some very good sense in what he says, and I particularly respect him for wishing to think well of all young ladies; it shows an amiable and a delicate mind. And he deserves better treatment than to be obliged to read any more of my works.

Do not be surprised at finding Uncle Henry acquainted with my having another ready for publication. I could not say No when he asked me, but he knows nothing more of it. You will not like it, so you need not be impatient. You may perhaps like the heroine, as she is almost too good for me.

Many thanks for your kind care for my health; I certainly have not been well for many weeks, and about a week ago I was very poorly. I have had a good deal of fever at times, and indifferent nights; but I am considerably better now, and am recovering my looks a little, which have been bad enough,—black and white, and every wrong color. I must not depend upon being ever very blooming again. Sickness is a dangerous indulgence at my time of life. Thank you for everything you tell me. I do not feel worthy of it by anything that I can say in return, but I assure you my pleasure in your letters is quite as great as ever, and I am interested and amused just as you could wish me. If there is a Miss *Marsden*, I perceive whom she will marry.

Evening.—I was languid and dull and very bad company when I wrote the above; I am better now, to my own feelings at least, and wish I may be more agreeable. We are going to have rain, and after that very pleasant genial weather, which will exactly do for me, as my saddle will then be completed, and air and exercise is what I want. Indeed, I shall be very glad when the event at Scarlets is over, the expectation of it keeps us in a worry, your grandmamma especially; she sits brooding over evils which cannot be remedied, and conduct impossible to be understood.

Now the reports from Keppel St. are rather better; little Harriot's headaches are abated, and Sir Evd. is satisfied with the effect of the mercury, and does not despair of a cure. The complaint I find is not considered incurable nowadays, provided the patient be young enough not to have the head hardened. The water in that case may be drawn off by mercury. But though this is a new idea to us, perhaps it may have been long familiar to you through your friend Mr. Scud. I hope his high renown is sustained by driving away William's cough.

Tell Wm. that Triggs is as beautiful and condescending as ever, and was so good as to dine with us to-day, and tell him that I often play at nines and think of him.

The Papillons came back on Friday night, but I have not seen them yet, as I do not venture to church. I cannot hear, however, but that they are the same Mr. P. and his sister they used to be. She has engaged a new maidservant in Mrs. Calker's room, whom she means to make also housekeeper under herself.

Old Philmore was buried yesterday, and I, by way of saying something to Triggs, observed that it had been a very handsome funeral; but his manner of reply made me suppose that it was not generally esteemed so. I can only be sure of one part being very handsome,—Triggs himself, walking behind in his green coat. Mrs. Philmore attended as chief mourner, in bombazine, made very short, and flounced with crape.

Tuesday.—I have had various plans as to this letter, but at last I have determined that Uncle Henry shall forward it from London. I want to see how Canterbury looks in the direction. When once Uncle H. has left us, I shall wish him with you. London has become a hateful place to him, and he is always depressed by the idea of it. I hope he will be in time for your sick. I am sure he must do that part of his duty as excellently as all the rest. He returned yesterday from Steventon, and was with us by breakfast, bringing Edward with him, only that Edwd. stayed to breakfast at Wyards. We had a pleasant family day, for the Altons dined with us, the last visit of the kind probably which she will be able to pay us for many a month.

I hope your own Henry is in France, and that you have heard from him; the passage once over, he will feel all happiness. I took my first ride yesterday, and liked it very much. I went up Mounter's Lane and round by where the new cottages are to be, and found the exercise and everything very pleasant; and I had the advantage of agreeable companions, as At. Cass. and Edward walked by my side. At. Cass. is such an excellent nurse, so assiduous and unwearied! But you know all that already.

Very affectionately yours,
J. AUSTEN.

Miss KNIGHT,
Godmersham Park, Canterbury.

LXXV.

CHAWTON, Sunday (Sept. 8, 1816).

MY DEAREST CASSANDRA,—I have borne the arrival of your letter to-day extremely well; anybody might have thought it was giving me pleasure. I am very glad you find so much to be satisfied with at Cheltenham. While the waters agree, everything else is trifling.

A letter arrived for you from Charles last Thursday. They are all safe and pretty well in Keppel St., the children decidedly better for Broadstairs; and he writes principally to ask when it will be convenient to us to receive Miss P., the little girls, and himself. They would be ready to set off in ten days from the time of his writing, to pay their visits in Hampshire and Berkshire, and he would prefer coming to Chawton first.

I have answered him, and said that we hoped it might suit them to wait till the last week in Septr., as we could not ask them sooner, either on your account or the want of room. I mentioned the 23rd as the probable day of your return. When you have once left Cheltenham, I shall grudge every half-day wasted on the road. If there were but a coach from Hungerford to Chawton! I have desired him to let me hear again soon.

He does not include a maid in the list to be accommodated; but if they bring one, as I suppose they will, we shall have no bed in the house even then for Charles himself,—let alone Henry. But what can we do?

We shall have the Gt. House quite at our command; it is to be cleared of the Papillons' servants in a day or two. They themselves have been hurried off into Essex to take possession,—not of a large estate left them by an uncle, but to scrape together all they can, I suppose, of the effects of a Mrs. Rawstorn, a rich old friend and cousin suddenly deceased, to whom they are joint executors. So there is a happy end of the Kentish Papillons coming here.

No morning service to-day, wherefore I am writing between twelve and one o'clock. Mr. Benn in the afternoon, and likewise more rain again, by the look and the sound of things. You left us in doubt of Mrs. Benn's situation, but she has bespoke her nurse.... The F. A.'s dined with us yesterday, and had fine weather both for coming and going home, which has hardly ever happened to them before. She is still unprovided with a housemaid.

Our day at Alton was very pleasant, venison quite right, children well behaved, and Mr. and Mrs. Digweed taking kindly to our charades and other games. I must also observe, for his mother's satisfaction, that Edward at my suggestion devoted himself very properly to the entertainment of Miss S. Gibson. Nothing was wanting except Mr. Sweeney; but he, alas! had been ordered away to London the day before. We had a beautiful walk home by moonlight.

Thank you, my back has given me scarcely any pain for many days. I have an idea that agitation does it as much harm as fatigue, and that I was ill at the time of your going from the very circumstance of your going. I am nursing myself up now into as beautiful a state as I can, because I hear that Dr. White means to call on me before he leaves the country.

Evening.—Frank and Mary and the children visited us this morning. Mr. and Mrs. Gibson are to come on the 23rd, and there is too much reason to fear they will stay above a week. Little George could tell me where you were gone to, as well as what you were to bring him, when I asked him the other day.

Sir Tho. Miller is dead. I treat you with a dead baronet in almost every letter.

So you have C. Craven among you, as well as the Duke of Orleans and Mr. Pocock. But it mortifies me that you have not added one to the stock of common acquaintance. Do pray meet with somebody belonging to yourself. I am quite weary of your knowing nobody.

Mrs. Digweed parts with both Hannah and old cook: the former will not give up her lover, who is a man of bad character; the latter is guilty only of being unequal to anything.

Miss Terry was to have spent this week with her sister, but as usual it is put off. My amiable friend knows the value of her company. I have not seen Anna since the day you left us; her father and brother visited her most days. Edward and Ben called here on Thursday. Edward was in his way to Selborne. We found him very agreeable. He is come back from France, thinking of the French as one could wish,—disappointed in everything. He did not go beyond Paris.

I have a letter from Mrs. Perigord; she and her mother are in London again. She speaks of France as a scene of general poverty and misery: no money, no trade, nothing to be got but by the innkeepers, and as to her own present prospects she is not much less melancholy than before.

I have also a letter from Miss Sharp, quite one of her letters; she has been again obliged to exert herself more than ever, in a more distressing, more harassed state, and has met with another excellent old physician and his wife, with every virtue under heaven, who takes to her and cures her from pure love and benevolence. Dr. and Mrs. Storer are their Mrs. and Miss Palmer—for they are at Bridlington. I am happy to say, however, that the sum of the account is better than usual. Sir William is returned; from Bridlington they go to Chevet, and she is to have a young governess under her.

I enjoyed Edward's company very much, as I said before, and yet I was not sorry when Friday came. It had been a busy week, and I wanted a few days' quiet and exemption from the thought and contrivancy which any sort of company gives. I often wonder how you can find time for what you do, in addition to the care of the house; and how good Mrs. West could have written such books and collected so many hard words, with all her family cares, is still more a matter of astonishment. Composition seems to me impossible with a head full of joints of mutton and doses of rhubarb.

Monday.—Here is a sad morning. I fear you may not have been able to get to the Pump. The two last days were very pleasant. I enjoyed them the more for your sake. But to-day it is really bad enough to make you all cross. I hope Mary will change her lodgings at the fortnight's end; I am sure, if you looked about well, you would find others in some odd corner to suit you better. Mrs. Potter charges for the name of the High St.

Success to the pianoforte! I trust it will drive you away. We hear now that there is to be no honey this year. Bad news for us. We must husband our present stock of mead, and I am sorry to perceive that our twenty gallons is very nearly out. I cannot comprehend how the fourteen gallons could last so long.

We do not much like Mr. Cooper's new sermons. They are fuller of regeneration and conversion than ever, with the addition of his zeal in the cause of the Bible Society.

Martha's love to Mary and Caroline, and she is extremely glad to find they like the pelisse. The Debarys are indeed odious! We are to see my brother to-morrow, but for only one night. I had no idea that he would care for the races without Edward. Remember me to all.

Yours very affectionately,
J. AUSTEN.

Miss AUSTEN, Post-Office, Cheltenham.

NOTE BY LORD BRABOURNE.

I insert here a letter of Jane Austen's written backwards, addressed to her niece "Cassy," daughter of Captain Charles Austen (afterwards Admiral) when a little girl.

LXXVI.

Ym raed Yssac,—I hsiw uoy a yppah wen raey. Ruoy xis snisuoc emac ereh yadretsey, dna dah hcae a eceip fo ekac. Siht si elttil Yssac's yadhtrib, dna ehs si eerht sraey dlo. Knarf sah nugeb gninrael Nital ew deef eht Nibor yreve gninrom. Yllas netfo seriuqne retfa uoy. Yllas Mahneb sah tog a wen neerg nwog. Teirrah Thgink semoc yreve yad ot daer ot Tnua Ardnassac. Doog eyb ym raed Yssac.

Tnua Ardnassac sdnes reh tseb evol, dna os ew od lla.

Ruoy etanoitceffa tnua,
Enaj Netsua.

Notwahc, Naj. 8.

Note by Lord Brabourne.

In January, 1817, she wrote of herself as better and able to walk into Alton, and hoped in the summer she should be able to walk back. In April her father in a note to Mrs. Lefroy says: "I was happy to have a good account of herself written by her own hand, in a letter from your Aunt Jane; but all who love, and that is all who know her, must be anxious on her account." We all know how well grounded that anxiety was, and how soon her relations had to lament over the loss of the dearest and brightest member of their family.

And now I come to the saddest letters of all, those which tell us of the end of that bright life, cut short just at the time when the world might have hoped that unabated intellectual vigor, supplemented by the experience brought by maturer years, would have produced works if possible even more fascinating than those with which she had already embellished the literature of her country. But it was not to be. The fiat had gone forth,—the ties which bound that sweet spirit to earth were to be severed, and a blank left, never to be filled in the family which her loved and loving presence had blessed, and where she had been so well and fondly appreciated. In the early spring of 1817 the unfavorable symptoms increased, and the failure of her health was too visible to be neglected. Still no apprehensions of immediate danger were entertained, and it is probable that when she left Chawton for Winchester in May, she did not recognize the fact that she was bidding a last farewell to "Home." Happy for her if it was so, for there are few things more melancholy than to look upon any beloved place or person with the knowledge that it is for "the last time." In all probability this grief was spared to Jane, for even after her arrival at Winchester she spoke and wrote as if recovery was hopeful; and I fancy that her relations were by no means aware that the end was so near.

Note by Lord Brabourne.

Cassandra's letters tell the tale of the event in words that require no addition from me. They are simple and affecting,—the words of one who had been stricken by a great grief, but whose religion stood her in good stead, and enabled her to bear it with fortitude. The firm and loving bond of union which had ever united the Austen family, naturally intensified their sorrow at the loss of one of their number, and that the one of whom they had been so proud as well as so fond. They laid her within the walls of the old cathedral which she had loved so much, and went sorrowfully back to their homes, with the feeling that nothing could replace to them the treasure they had lost. And most heavily of all must the blow have fallen upon the only sister, the correspondent, the companion, the other self of Jane, who had to return alone to the desolate home, and to the mother to whose comforts the two had hitherto ministered together, but who would henceforward have her alone on whom to rely....

Letters from Miss Cassandra Austen to her niece Miss Knight, after the death of her sister Jane, July 18, 1817.

LXXVII.

WINCHESTER, Sunday.

MY DEAREST FANNY,—Doubly dear to me now for her dear sake whom we have lost. She did love you most sincerely, and never shall I forget the proofs of love you gave her during her illness in writing those kind, amusing letters at a time when I know your feelings would have dictated so different a style. Take the only reward I can give you in the assurance that your benevolent purpose was answered; you did contribute to her enjoyment.

Even your last letter afforded pleasure. I merely cut the seal and gave it to her; she opened it and read it herself, afterwards she gave it to me to read, and then talked to me a little and not uncheerfully of its contents, but there was then a languor about her which prevented her taking the same interest in anything she had been used to do.

Since Tuesday evening, when her complaint returned, there was a visible change, she slept more and much more comfortably; indeed, during the last eight-and-forty hours she was more asleep than awake. Her looks altered and she fell away, but I perceived no material diminution of strength, and though I was then hopeless of a recovery, I had no suspicion how rapidly my loss was approaching.

I have lost a treasure, such a sister, such a friend as never can have been surpassed. She was the sun of my life, the gilder of every pleasure, the soother of every sorrow; I had not a thought concealed from her, and it is as if I had lost a part of myself. I loved her only too well,—not better than she deserved, but

I am conscious that my affection for her made me sometimes unjust to and negligent of others; and I can acknowledge, more than as a general principle, the justice of the Hand which has struck this blow.

You know me too well to be at all afraid that I should suffer materially from my feelings; I am perfectly conscious of the extent of my irreparable loss, but I am not at all overpowered and very little indisposed,—nothing but what a short time, with rest and change of air, will remove. I thank God that I was enabled to attend her to the last, and amongst my many causes of self-reproach I have not to add any wilful neglect of her comfort.

She felt herself to be dying about half an hour before she became tranquil and apparently unconscious. During that half-hour was her struggle, poor soul! She said she could not tell us what she suffered, though she complained of little fixed pain. When I asked her if there was anything she wanted, her answer was she wanted nothing but death, and some of her words were: "God grant me patience, pray for me, oh, pray for me!" Her voice was affected, but as long as she spoke she was intelligible.

I hope I do not break your heart, my dearest Fanny, by these particulars; I mean to afford you gratification whilst I am relieving my own feelings. I could not write so to anybody else; indeed you are the only person I have written to at all, excepting your grandmamma,—it was to her, not your Uncle Charles, I wrote on Friday.

Immediately after dinner on Thursday I went into the town to do an errand which your dear aunt was anxious about. I returned about a quarter before six, and found her recovering from faintness and oppression; she got so well as to be able to give me a minute account of her seizure, and when the clock struck six she was talking quietly to me.

I cannot say how soon afterwards she was seized again with the same faintness, which was followed by the sufferings she could not describe; but Mr. Lyford had been sent for, had applied something to give her ease, and she was in a state of quiet insensibility by seven o'clock at the latest. From that time till half-past four, when she ceased to breathe, she scarcely moved a limb, so that we have every reason to think, with gratitude to the Almighty, that her sufferings were over. A slight motion of the head with every breath remained till almost the last. I sat close to her with a pillow in my lap to assist in supporting her head, which was almost off the bed, for six hours; fatigue made me then resign my place to Mrs. J. A. for two hours and a half, when I took it again, and in about an hour more she breathed her last.

I was able to close her eyes myself, and it was a great gratification to me to render her those last services. There was nothing convulsed which gave the idea of pain in her look; on the contrary, but for the continual motion of the head she gave one the idea of a beautiful statue, and even now, in her coffin, there is such a sweet, serene air over her countenance as is quite pleasant to contemplate.

This day, my dearest Fanny, you have had the melancholy intelligence, and I know you suffer severely, but I likewise know that you will apply to the fountain-head for consolation, and that our merciful God is never deaf to such prayers as you will offer.

The last sad ceremony is to take place on Thursday morning; her dear remains are to be deposited in the cathedral. It is a satisfaction to me to think that they are to lie in a building she admired so much; her precious soul, I presume to hope, reposes in a far superior mansion. May mine one day be reunited to it!

Your dear papa, your Uncle Henry, and Frank and Edwd. Austen, instead of his father, will attend. I hope they will none of them suffer lastingly from their pious exertions. The ceremony must be over before ten o'clock, as the cathedral service begins at that hour, so that we shall be at home early in the day, for there will be nothing to keep us here afterwards.

Your Uncle James came to us yesterday, and is gone home to-day. Uncle H. goes to Chawton to-morrow morning; he has given every necessary direction here, and I think his company there will do good. He returns to us again on Tuesday evening.

I did not think to have written a long letter when I began, but I have found the employment draw me on, and I hope I shall have been giving you more pleasure than pain. Remember me kindly to Mrs. J. Bridges (I am so glad she is with you now), and give my best love to Lizzie and all the others.

I am, my dearest Fanny,
Most affectionately yours,
CASS. ELIZ. AUSTEN.

I have said nothing about those at Chawton, because I am sure you hear from your papa.

LXXVIII.

CHAWTON, Tuesday (July 29, 1817).

MY DEAREST FANNY,—I have just read your letter for the third time, and thank you most sincerely for every kind expression to myself, and still more warmly for your praises of her who I believe was better known to you than to any human being besides myself. Nothing of the sort could have been more gratifying to me than the manner in which you write of her; and if the dear angel is conscious of what passes here, and is not above all earthly feelings, she may perhaps receive pleasure in being so mourned. Had she been the survivor, I can fancy her speaking of you in almost the same terms. There are certainly many points of strong resemblance in your characters; in your intimate acquaintance with each other, and your mutual strong affection, you were counterparts.

Thursday was not so dreadful a day to me as you imagined. There was so much necessary to be done that there was no time for additional misery. Everything was conducted with the greatest tranquillity, and but that I was determined I would see the last, and therefore was upon the listen, I should not have known when they left the house. I watched the little mournful procession the length of the street; and when it turned from my sight, and I had lost her forever, even then I was not overpowered, nor so much agitated as I am now in writing of it. Never was human being more sincerely mourned by those who attended her remains than was this dear creature. May the sorrow with which she is parted with on earth be a prognostic of the joy with which she is hailed in heaven!

I continue very tolerably well,—much better than any one could have supposed possible, because I certainly have had considerable fatigue of body as well as anguish of mind for months back; but I really am well, and I hope I am properly grateful to the Almighty for having been so supported. Your grandmamma, too, is much better than when I came home.

I did not think your dear papa appeared unwell, and I understand that he seemed much more comfortable after his return from Winchester than he had done before. I need not tell you that he was a great comfort to me; indeed, I can never say enough of the kindness I have received from him and from every other friend.

I get out of doors a good deal, and am able to employ myself. Of course those employments suit me best which leave me most at leisure to think of her I have lost, and I do think of her in every variety of circumstance,—in our happy hours of confidential intercourse, in the cheerful family party which she so ornamented, in her sick-room, on her death-bed, and as (I hope) an inhabitant of heaven. Oh, if I may one day be reunited to her there! I know the time must come when my mind will be less engrossed by her idea, but I do not like to think of it. If I think of her less as on earth, God grant that I may never cease to reflect on her as inhabiting heaven, and never cease my humble endeavors (when it shall please God) to join her there.

In looking at a few of the precious papers which are now my property I have found some memorandums, amongst which she desires that one of her gold chains may be given to her god-daughter Louisa, and a lock of her hair be set for you. You can need no assurance, my dearest Fanny, that every request of your beloved aunt will be sacred with me. Be so good as to say whether you prefer a brooch or ring. God bless you, my dearest Fanny.

Believe me, most affectionately yours,
CASS. ELIZTH. AUSTEN.

Miss KNIGHT,
Godmersham Park, Canterbury.

THE END.

CPSIA information can be obtained
at www.ICGtesting.com
Printed in the USA
LVHW030736191119
637838LV00001B/277/P